THE ELIZABETHAN NATION

Joel Hurstfield

THE ELIZABETHAN NATION

Joel Hurstfield

BRITISH BROADCASTING CORPORATION

© 1964 *Joel Hurstfield*

Published by the British Broadcasting Corporation
*35 Marylebone High Street, London W*1
Printed in England at the Shenval Press,
London, Hertford and Harlow
No. 5918

CONTENTS

ACKNOWLEDGEMENTS

I owe to Miss Jean Rowntree both the original suggestion for this book and her valuable critical encouragement throughout. I am indebted also to Dr A. G. R. Smith of Glasgow University, to Mr A. G. Petti of the English Department of University College and to Jennifer Hurstfield for reading and commenting on the original typescript. I gratefully acknowledge the permission granted by the editors of *History Today* to reproduce a passage from my article 'England in the year 1564', and by Dr R. B. Outhwaite for a passage from his doctoral dissertation on Elizabethan Finance. I never lose sight of my debt to the students of London University who, for nearly two decades, have joined me in a study of this period; and I hope that they may perhaps find in this book some echoes of our shared experience.

J. H.

Illustrations are reproduced by courtesy of:

Bodleian Library, page 51; British Museum, pages 50, 53, 56 and 58; Mrs Dent-Brocklehurst, page 55 (top); The Burrell Collection, Glasgow Art Gallery and Museum, page 61 (top r.); Cambridge University Press (from *An Historical Geography of England before A.D. 1800* edt. by H. C. Darby), inside back cover; City Library, Exeter, page 57; John R. Freeman, page 63; Longmans, Green & Co, page 49; National Buildings Record, page 52; National Maritime Museum, page 54; National Portrait Gallery, pages 55 (bottom) and 59; Radio Times Hulton Picture Library, page 62; Marquess of Salisbury, cover; Society of Antiquaries, page 64; Victoria and Albert Museum, pages 60 and 61 (top l. and bottom).

Photographs were taken by G. Ashburner (page 58), Z. Wegner (page 55) and John Webb (cover, pages 27 and 56).

THE RADIO PROGRAMMES

The Elizabethan Nation is a new venture in broadcasting which offers the listener a detailed view of an important period of English history. It is made up of two main series and two associated series.

Elizabethan Government and Society: Third Network, weekly, from 11 January to 8 March.
Mondays, 11.15 to 11.45 p.m.

Eight lectures delivered to first and second year history and English students at the University of East Anglia by Joel Hurstfield, Astor Professor of English History in the University of London, in November 1964; and one question-and-answer programme recorded from questions asked by students and answered by Professor Hurstfield at the end of each lecture.

The course examines the politics and society of the Elizabethan nation in the light of recent historical research. In his opening lecture, Professor Hurstfield asks: Who were the Elizabethans, what did they stand for, and how did their system evolve? In the following lectures he considers their social structure and political system; the established church, and the Puritan and Catholic opposition to it. He discusses their political theories, foreign policy, and attitude to parliament and law; and ends with an examination of the decline of the Elizabethan political order. The course is illustrated from tracts, speeches, political writings, public and private correspondence, and the writings of poets, essayists and playwrights.

These lectures are offered to the listener in the belief that a great many people who did not themselves have a university education will welcome this opportunity of following a series which is part of a degree course in History and English, and that students in other universities will be glad to hear an established broadcaster, who is also an outstanding authority on his subject.

Elizabethan Culture and Ideas: Third Network, weekly, from 14 January to 11 March.
Thursdays, 7.00 to 7.30 p.m.

Nine programmes by a succession of different speakers, broadcast from the studio, on special aspects of the period – for example, its ideas on art, science, usury, poverty, or the physical world. Some of the programmes will be illustrated by examples of Elizabethan music and dialect, and all of them will be based on contemporary texts illustrated by readings.

Painting of the Month main series: Third Network, monthly.
1 January, 5 February, 5 March.
Fridays, 6.45 to 7.05 p.m.
Repeated in the Home Service on Sundays,
3 January, 7 February, 7 March, 10.10 to 10.30 p.m.

David Piper, Director of the National Portrait Gallery, discusses paintings of the fifteenth and sixteenth centuries.

Painting of the Month supplementary series: Third Network, monthly.
15 January, 19 February, 19 March. Fridays, 6.45 to 7.05 p.m.
Repeated in the Home Service on Sundays,
17 January, 21 February, 21 March, 10.10 to 10.30 p.m.

Sir John Summerson, Keeper of Sir John Soane's Museum, talks about three country houses of the period – Kirby in Northamptonshire, Hardwick Hall in Derbyshire, and Hatfield in Hertfordshire.

These programmes form part of a series on the development of Art in Britain based on examples which are accessible to the public. They are planned for subscribers to the BBC's project *Painting of the Month*, who receive reproductions of the works discussed (paintings in colour), together with background notes and black and white illustrations: the material is sent out quarterly. For further details, write to Painting of the Month, BBC Publications, 35 Marylebone High Street, London, W.1.

*

During the first quarter of 1965 there will thus be twenty-four programmes, at different times and on different evenings, focusing on a single period of English history and society. Each series is a unity in itself, but listeners who hear the broadcasts, read this book, and visit the galleries and country houses, will have a detailed and up-to-date picture of the politics and culture of Elizabethan England which it would be difficult to acquire in any other way.

I

The Elizabethan People in

1558

Amongst the many bold claims made by Elizabeth's
father, Henry VIII, the boldest is enshrined in a famous
statute. 'This realm of England,' runs the preamble to
the Act in Restraint of Appeals of 1533, 'is an empire.'
The word empire had not yet acquired in those days the
nineteenth-century overtones of civilising missions,
(with all that was good and evil in them) or colonial
exploitation. To Henry VIII and to the English parliamentarians, empire meant independence. In declaring
that England was an empire, Henry VIII was issuing
a declaration of independence: England was a self-
governing nation, free from any kind of exterior control
by any authority. In this context he was thinking of the
Pope. But his language and policy left no doubt that if
the Emperor Charles V (who was also King of Spain)
wished to pull some of the papal chestnuts out of the fire,
then this was an announcement of defiance to him too.

The declaration of empire of 1533 is as important in
English history as the Declaration of Independence of
1776 is in the history of America or the Declaration of
the Rights of Man of 1789 is in the history of France.
Yet, unlike these, it is by now largely forgotten. But to
Tudor Englishmen its scope and content were major
elements in their political thinking. The period which
followed, and especially the four and a half decades
which comprised Elizabeth's reign, represent a long,
almost unbroken, struggle to fulfil and enforce this

first assertion by Englishmen of their sovereign rights as an independent nation. It proved a declaration easier to proclaim than to sustain.

For all Europe lay under the shadow of the Reformation; and England more than any other country was tossed violently about by swiftly changing winds. Henry VIII himself knew well that the revolution he had carried through was uneasily poised and unstable, and that the time-servers who had bowed to his authority would be willing to serve other times under his successors. Such is the risk inherent in all revolutions; and it was the greater in this case for it was a revolution in both church and state.

Where would it all end? Henry himself saw soon enough that in putting the English Bible in the hands of the masses he was placing gunpowder on every street corner and in every tavern in the land. For the Bible offered little to comfort the established order and much to encourage its destruction. He had wanted a religious revolution only in the sense that he wished to overthrow the acknowledged head of the church, the Pope, and replace him by another head, himself; but in doctrine and ceremonial he hoped – mistakenly, as it turned out – that the church would stand where it had always stood. He wanted a revolution in the state in that the crown would gain immensely in economic power from the confiscation of the large, rich territories of the church, and he wanted too the vast accession of political sovereignty which the headship of the church carried with it. But he wanted no social revolution, the kind developing in north Germany in the wake of rapid religious change. Henry VIII was a revolutionary who was suspicious of all revolt. He believed – as many others have since then vainly believed – that he who starts a revolution can tell it where to stop. The revolution which Henry inaugurated in the Reformation Parliament of 1529 to 1536 moved forward inexorably with gathering momentum, a momentum which had only spent itself when the head of a king fell, more than a century later, in 1649.

It was in this shadow of Reformation and revolution that Elizabeth and the Elizabethans were born. And neither she nor they ever knew stability again for the rest of their lives. A child born in 1533, the year of Elizabeth's birth, would have little chance of ever reaching the advanced age of 69 at which she died. He would indeed be fortunate if he reached half that age. But even if he died at thirty-five he would have seen social changes of a degree and significance far greater than any witnessed by men who lived twice his years in preceding centuries. But these social changes have been obscured for historians by the more dramatic episodes of the Reformation. Social change lacks the impact and emphasis of religious conflict yet its effect is often much wider. For whereas in any community there is a considerable body of religious neutralism – the religious storms blow themselves out over their heads – these people can never declare their neutrality to economic change. For it gives them no choice. If we were so bold as to try to summarise that change in a sentence, we should say that there was an economic and social revolution resulting from the pressure throughout western Europe of a growing, thrusting population upon scarce land and scarce resources. In short, as the population rose, the land and the food began to give out.

All this growth of population must seem surprising in the light of what one knows about the appalling conditions of life, the over-crowded houses, the grim hazards of childbirth, the primitive hit or miss – usually miss – medicine, the plagues, the famines, the wars, the capital penalties for trivial crimes. But we who live in the twentieth century, in another and greater phase of a population expansion, should not be surprised. For it is one of the great social paradoxes of our time that where the standard of living is lowest population is rising fastest. Nature is generous at a child's birth even if she then withholds her bounty for the rest of his life. The human frame has the capacity to keep alive in the most desperate and barren conditions. But it is only just alive. We should not forget that for a large part of their lives Tudor Englishmen lived in sickness and pain and sorrow, and with no great expectation of long life or good living.

The rich of course lived richly, and the poor at the lowest standard of subsistence. But plague and sudden death acknowledged no class distinctions; and the characteristic portraits of eminent Elizabethans in the full panoply of wealth and office, with one of their hands resting upon a skull, served to remind them and us of the frail mortality of man, that, in the words of the seventeenth-century poet, James Shirley,

> Sceptre and crown
> Must tumble down
> And in the dust be equal made.

Even after this long interval of time, there is a sharp poignancy for the historian as he comes upon their letters of condolence with their resigned acceptance that this world was but a brief resting place of suffering on the brink of eternity.

Equally pathetic were their efforts to ward off disease. 'There is to be observed three things', wrote John Johnson, the London merchant, then at Calais, to a friend, at the time of the terrible sweating sickness of 1551, 'that is, the sweat being begun, no air to be suffered to come in to the bed, but yet not to be kept over hot; to drink as little as may be . . . and the third and principal thing is to be kept from sleep so long as sleep is desired in the twenty-four hours . . . for he that sleepeth, dieth'. We do not know whether this crude, if not positively harmful, remedy was ever applied to Johnson's brother Otwell. All that we know is that Otwell on 8 July, 1551, wrote his customary business letter to his brother, and in the early hours of July 10th he was dead.

But in fact, although many people caught the sweating sickness or some other infection, most people did not die from these visitations. And Tudor England knew nothing comparable to the Black Death of the Middle Ages when half the population of a village might be wiped out. Since the middle of the fifteenth century the fall in population, which had been going on for a century, had been arrested and soon numbers were rising. Even so, it is doubtful whether on the eve of Elizabeth's accession there were more than three or four million Englishmen, or more than five at the end of the reign.

But when population pressures are being exerted it is not numbers which matter but the relationship between numbers and the resources to employ and feed them. England in 1558 was a backward country: backward not simply in comparison with its conditions today, but backward even when compared with some other countries of the sixteenth century, notably the Netherlands, France, North Germany and North Italy. Such industry as she had was domestic industry, mainly the spinning and weaving of cloth, for finishing in more advanced centres, primarily in the Low Countries. Much of the English textile industry was conducted as a bye-employment, a country occupation during the intervals of work on the land.

Her agricultural processes had improved as compared with earlier centuries but in no respects sufficiently to feed the many more who looked to the land. Moreover agriculture was under strain for two additional reasons. Some land, especially in the midlands, had during the first half of the century been converted from corn to pasture: the wool to feed the apparently insatiable textile industry yielded higher profits than the corn to feed human mouths. Meanwhile less men were wanted to tend sheep than to grow corn. 'The sheep,' cried Sir Thomas More, 'that were wont to be so meek and tame, and so small eaters, now, as I hear say, be become so great devourers and so wild that they eat up and swallow down the very men themselves.' But at the same time some new towns, stimulated by the textile industry, were growing fast, while London most impressively had passed the 100,000 mark. All this made for a distortion of the traditional economy of England, although it had, of course, long, long before ceased to be simply a subsistence economy.

Beggary walked abroad in the land. To Bishop Ridley, the future martyr, it walked in the form of Christ rejected: hence his plea to William Cecil, at that time in the service of Edward vi. 'Good Master Cecil,' he wrote in 1552, 'I must be a suitor unto you in our good Master Christ's cause. I beseech you to be good to Him. The matter is, Sir, alas! He hath lain too long abroad (as you do know) without lodging in the streets of London, both hungry, naked and cold. Now, thanks be to Almighty God, the citizens are willing to refresh Him, and to give Him both meat, drink, clothing and firing. But, alas! Sir, they lack lodging for Him.' So Ridley appealed for the use of the 'wide, large, empty house of the King's Majesty's, called Bridewell, that would wonderfully well serve to lodge Christ in, if he might find such good friends in the Court to procure in his cause'. Bridewell was indeed granted. But it proved more popular with the City Fathers than with the inmates. Organised as it was on the still prevailing assumption that if men were not at work, it was because they chose idleness, its regimen was oppressive and deterrent. But the Tudors were learning the elements of social welfare and, as a later chapter will show, were making significant progress.

But what happens when men grow faster than the means to feed or clothe them, and when money becomes more plentiful than goods? Those of us who have lived through war conditions know, from our own experiences, exactly what happens. A nation at war diverts a large part of her manpower and materials to non-productive purposes. As a result essentials become scarce, prices rise and, as happened during the First and Second World Wars, governments are forced to impose rationing systems to reduce the pressure of money on goods. The notion of a rationing system – other than striking clumsily at obvious hoarders – would not have occurred to a Tudor government; or if it had it would have been well beyond the remotest prospects of enforcement. So prices rose; and by the middle of the sixteenth century the government faced with bewilderment and dismay the full blast of a runaway inflation, until then without parallel in English history.

We do not need Henry VIII's devaluation and de-basement of the coinage to explain these startling and revolutionary processes, although a depreciated currency certainly played its part. But when the currency was restored in 1561 the processes of inflation continued, albeit at a slower pace. Nor will the influx of precious metals from the New World carry us a good deal further, although again it contributed to these upward processes. Our principal explanation lies in the fact that population outdistanced supplies; and, to confirm this, we notice that inflation did not slacken until the 1630s, that is until the upward thrust of population itself slackened.

Meanwhile, in 1551, at the height of inflation, an already unstable situation flared up into crisis. For in that year the long boom in English cloth exports at last collapsed. The Antwerp market reached saturation. The warehouses of the English merchants were stuffed to capacity. The cloth-workers were laid off. On top of that the harvest failed disastrously. Unemployment, poverty, inflation struck at English society together; and then in 1557, under Mary, there came the renewed troubles of war, a pointless war in France as a satellite of Spain. The war lasted on until her death in 1558.

15

Eleven years before, Henry VIII's reign had ended in 1547 with depression and war. The short reign of his son, Edward VI, had ended in 1553 with political corruption and economic confusion. His daughter Mary, reigning also for only five years, saw her ministers strenuously work to purify the system and introduce some measure of reform. But with lofty motives and misguided passion, she drove forward for doctrinal purity as well, heedless of the cost to her subjects and her name. And now, on 17 November, 1558, Elizabeth I entered upon her inheritance, burdened with a tainted title, a divided and impoverished people and a foreign war.

In thinking of this nation in the year 1558, historians are too much inclined to look upon the situation from the viewpoint of the central government. Unconsciously we postulate a twentieth-century nation with an effective centralised government, with unified communications and direction, with a common experience and a common aim. Of course, England was a nation, more unified than Germany or Italy or even France. But it was still a land of village communities, small and widely scattered towns, slow communications, sometimes rendered completely non-existent by storm or flood. Most occupations were rural occupations. The medieval manor survived in many parts of the country as an economic and administrative unit but with villein tenure almost a thing of the past. Tin was mined in Cornwall, iron smelted in Sussex and the Forest of Dean; coal mined in Durham. These were all country occupations. Some of the textile processes were done in towns; but many of these towns were in fact overgrown villages. There were important cities too with ancient histories like York, Bristol, Salisbury. But they too were small. Norwich the second largest city in the kingdom had a population of less than 20,000. Most Englishmen were countrymen.

But if nearly all Englishmen were countrymen following the rhythms of nature under the same English sky, their horizons in most cases extended no further than a cluster of villages or perhaps the shire in which they lived. They were not only countrymen, they were *county-men*. Local loyalties could be intense, regional differences profound. Lancashire and Kent differed greatly from each other in their climate, their economy, the balance between the old faith and the new, their culture. Somerset differed from Cumberland and both counties differed from Cornwall. All three differed from Wales. Since 1536 Wales had been submitted to an intensified process of Anglicisation, broken up into shires, represented in the Parliament at London, her language sentenced to extinction. In many of these processes of Anglicisation, the Welsh governing classes gladly co-operated. But their language stoutly resisted the threat of an alien tongue; and their native Bible, their music and poetry joined in the defence, a defence which held firm on into our own day, until the more seductive pressures of the mass media began to sap its resistance.

The process of Anglicisation was applied to Ireland too, but with a heavy and bloody hand and with ever diminishing chances of success, especially when alien domination by England became identified with an alien and new Protestant religion imposed upon an ancient Catholic people. And the position became irretrievable at the end of the sixteenth century when Ireland became a military side-show in a greater struggle between England and Spain. Scotland was a separate and independent kingdom, but it formed part of the French imperial dream, and, as such, a permanent strategic threat to England. But Scotland was weak, a prey to baronial feud and social disorder, the crown itself threatened by faction. She desperately needed internal peace and, until it was achieved, lay in constant risk of foreign intervention.

The impressive thing about this small realm of

England was its immense regional diversity. This means that when we speak of the Elizabethan nation we are always conscious that it was a nation still in the making. If a time should come when there was severe internal social crisis or successful foreign intervention, she could, as a nation, still be broken apart, especially if ideology lent fire to the sword. That was the experience of France during the so-called Wars of Religion, which lasted on during the greater part of Elizabeth's reign. The middle years of the sixteenth century bred a troubled generation all over Europe. Englishmen were perhaps less troubled than most.

In many ways these Elizabethan Englishmen formed a hopeful generation, full of vitality and promise. Nowhere was this better displayed than in the bold – if hardly beautiful – verses of that fine scholar, Roger Ascham, tutor to the Princess Elizabeth:

> Rejoice England, be glad and merry,
> Truth overcometh thine enemies all.
> The Scot, the Frenchman, the Pope and heresy,
> Overcomed by Truth, have had a fall.
> Stick to the Truth, and evermore thou shall
> Through Christ, King Henry, the Book and the Bow,
> All manner of enemies quite overthrow.

To Ascham, literature was part of the armoury in defence of Tudor Anglicanism, the just cause. But to Ascham also, and to many other Englishmen like Sir Thomas More, Dean Colet, Sir John Cheke the good life and good government were best to be found in classical literature and the classical way of life, re-moulded in Christian terms. Hence these men were called Christian humanists. But the movement had a long medieval ancestry and it, too, was a European phenomenon. The classical – and pagan – concept of a man-centred world in which man could look forward to an infinity of progress towards self-expression and self-fulfilment in this world was somehow merged, in their writings, with a Christ-centred world in which small, insignificant man passed briefly through this vale of tears on toward the infinity of a Christian heaven. The compromise while it lasted, especially in the half century before Elizabeth's accession, was a powerful influence in Tudor culture. But it did not last. The compromise showed signs of strain in Elizabeth's reign as we see in the work of Ralegh, Marlowe, Donne and Shakespeare himself. It is this tension between the classical and Christian attitudes in Elizabethan literature which added immensely to its colour, originality, beauty and force.

In the early days of humanism Englishmen found their masters and inspirers abroad, in northern Italy especially, and in great European scholars like Erasmus of Rotterdam who, for a time, lived and taught in this country. The same was true in the plastic arts where for a good part of the sixteenth century it was foreign artists and craftsmen who set their impress upon English culture, men like Torregiano, Holbein, Lucas Heere. But in music native traditions were already strong; the Chapel Royal stimulated and patronised succeeding generations of composers of sacred music, as did Henry VIII –something of a composer himself – in the secular sphere. So too did the noble and gentry households give employment and encouragement to musicians. Matthew Parker, Elizabeth's Archbishop of Canterbury, a man of considerable culture, employed in his palace the composer Thomas Whythorne, who was incidentally the author of the first modern English autobiography. If, in literature, many of the best minds were diverted towards theological controversy, we should not forget that the English Bible, Foxe's Book of Martyrs, the Book of Common Prayer, the vivid, racy sermons of men like Hugh Latimer formed the crucible of English prose out of which there came the virile, melodious, rhythmic English of the great Elizabethans. The surprising thing is that, although English poetry had produced in the first half of the sixteenth century men like Skelton, Wyatt and Surrey, there was little to suggest, either in poetry or the drama, the dazzling accomplishments of the age that were in prospect.

The culture we have been describing flourished under the vigorous patronage of crown, aristocracy and middle class. That same patronage was to be found in the field of government. The supreme importance of the House of Lords was itself just beginning to wane before the rising prestige and self-confidence of the House of Commons, those few hundred representatives of the shires and boroughs of England and Wales. But in the shires themselves some eminent nobleman, a Duke of Norfolk, an Earl of Northumberland, an Earl of Derby continued to exercise enormous influence upon local policy and the appointment to office. If it could be said in Northumberland that they knew no Prince but a Percy, then it might have been said in Norfolk that they knew no Prince but a Howard.

At quarter sessions members of the upper and middle classes of the shires would meet as justices of the peace to impose law and order as well as to administer local government, under instruction from London – instruction, it must be said, that was more often given than obeyed. For the country had a strong sense of local patriotism and local interest which, even after centuries of efforts by the monarchy to make its writ run throughout the land, survived and resisted the controlling impulse of the capital. Yet this regional self-determinism and isolation was passing away; and one of the forces making for a sense of nationhood was Parliament. We must not exaggerate its importance. It had to be called for legislation and for certain forms of taxation; but otherwise it was not essential. If the crown did not require new laws or fresh taxation it had no reason to summon Parliament, and no authority or law could make it do so. Often years went by without an assembly of

Parliament. Even when it sat, which was infrequently and for only a few weeks, it exercised influence rather than power; and had not even influence over the appointment to ministerial office. That lay exclusively with royal patronage. But Parliament was a place where men from all parts of the kingdom gathered and talked and became aware of their common interests – not all of them coinciding with the interests of the crown. By 1558 they had gained considerable legislative experience in helping to carry through a Protestant Reformation under Henry VIII and carrying it further under Edward VI, as well as carrying through a counter-Reformation under Mary. These men were not elected by anything resembling the democratic processes of modern times. They came in by patronage, local pressures and, on occasion, quite simply by sharp practice. But, once in, they became an important channel of communication between the nation and the government, an instrument for unifying the whole nation. But the greatest instrument for union was the monarchy itself.

Under Henry VIII the monarchy acquired unparalleled powers and prestige in church and state. Those powers had, in practice, suffered some attrition under Edward VI and Mary, with faction dominant under the one and fanaticism under the other. The monarchy was weakened in its economic resources and its popular esteem. But the forms and machinery of monarchy survived, as well as a good deal of its pomp and fame, The question which faced statesmen in 1558 was: how far would Elizabeth Tudor, this young and inexperienced woman of twenty-five, succeed in a task in which one nearly twice her years had so tragically failed?

II

The Dream of Order

1558-70

'To no Prince is done more honour and reverence than to the King and Queen of England', wrote Sir Thomas Smith, Elizabeth's ambassador in Paris, in 1565. He was writing his *De Republica Anglorum*, a famous study of English government and society; and in this chapter was explaining the nature of the English monarchy. The ambassador could not resist the temptation to point out that his fellow countrymen fully understood the niceties of diplomatic immunity. Foreigners, he wrote, were exempt from these rigours of formality; 'For all strangers be suffered there and in all places to use the manner of their country.' 'Such,' he complacently observes, 'is the civility of our nation.' But Englishmen sustained the high pomp of majesty. 'No man,' he said, 'speaketh to the Prince nor serveth at the table but in adoration and kneeling, all persons of the realm be bareheaded before him, insomuch that in the chamber of presence where the cloth of estate is set, no man dare walk; yea though the Prince be not there, no man dare tarry there but bareheaded.'

Here indeed we have the divinity which doth hedge a crown. But how far did this conform to reality? Was Elizabeth Tudor the divine virgin who was at once proclaimed a goddess by all Englishmen? It is all too easy to assume that this was a natural and logical development, and to forget the experiences of other women rulers. Being a woman was a grave handicap to Queen

Matilda, of no help to Mary Tudor and a very ambiguous asset to Mary, Queen of Scots. Many Parliamentarians long believed that Elizabeth's virginity gravely handicapped them as much as their queen, for it imperilled the Protestant succession. So historians are confronted with a new question. By whom and with what means was an initial handicap turned into the great symbol of virtuous godhead? By whom and with what means was the cult of personality focused on Elizabeth.

We are only just beginning to understand how this came about. Miss Frances Yates of the Warburg Institute, Dr R. G. Strong of the National Portrait Gallery and others have investigated the numerous techniques of portraiture, poetry, pageantry by means of which the popular image was created until the whole campaign of majesty was carried forward by its own momentum. But the Cult of the Virgin had long been an essential and important feature of medieval Christianity, and it was only discarded in England at the time of the Reformation. It may be true, as has been suggested, that the void was partly filled with the new cult of the new virgin. But there is nothing to suggest that Elizabeth resolved from the outset to remain unmarried, and clung to this resolution with a devout constancy. What is perfectly clear is that she exploited her femininity in every possible sphere. It became in its own right a political force of considerable proportions.

The problem is a very complex one. Elizabeth was a woman of high emotions – how could she be otherwise with such a father and such a mother? – but her throne inhibited her. It was this inhibition which sterilised her long emotional entanglement with the Earl of Leicester, and which later made hopeless the extraordinary courtship of the Duke of Alençon, a courtship which seemed anything but extraordinary to the queen. If these marriage projects seemed just possible to the queen, all the rest were impossible. She became a virgin of necessity and her necessity became a virtue.

So it came about that, when the battle with the Spaniards was finally joined in 1585, her virginity was already the symbol that England would remain inviolate before the onslaught of hostile powers; and in 1588 the apotheosis was complete.

She was helped by another major influence. During the Elizabethan period the kind of picture that Englishmen liked most of all to possess was portraiture. Men like Zuccari were attracted to England primarily for their portraits. Wealthy Englishmen sought after portraits painted abroad. Later Nicholas Hilliard and Isaac Oliver brilliantly developed English miniature painting. Meanwhile pictures of the queen were in heavy demand; and a native industry grew up to meet it, not always to the taste of the queen. She gave orders that these debased images should be consigned to the flames. No such command was issued about the excruciating verse disseminated by self-appointed laureates. What pleasure they gave to contemporaries – or to the queen – it is hard to tell; but they are helpful to the historian, for they provide some measure of the broad compass of her popular fame. We meet a more charming example of these things in the lines, accidentally preserved, of a schoolboy, John Slye, who scribbled on his copy of *Caesar*:

> The rose is redd, the leves are grene
> God save Elizabeth our noble Quene.

Sir Thomas Smith, whose proud words we quoted at the beginning of this chapter, pondered, elsewhere in his book, the whole question of a woman ruler. He believed, as did all his countrymen, that a woman's place was at home. But a queen regnant, he said, was different. If the right of inheritance passed to a woman then, in the interests of justice and security, it could not be challenged. It is of course understood, he added, that these

24

rulers would make up for their own deficiencies by the counsel of experienced men. A body of sage statesmen, apparently, was also needed to hedge a crown against the inherent weaknesses of feminine rule.

It sounds as if the ambassador was trying hard to convince himself. For, it must be admitted, during these first seven years of her rule Elizabeth had not shown herself very amenable to the guidance of sage statesmen, nor could she always recognise good advice when she was given it. To many of her ministers her vacillation was intolerable. 'It maketh me weary of my life, . . .' wrote the same Thomas Smith later on (when he was Secretary of State to the queen); 'I can neither get the other letters signed,' he said, 'nor the letter already signed . . . sent away, but day by day and hour by hour deferred till "anon", "soon" and "tomorrow".' At no time, indeed, was there a greater need for wise heads and cool spirits. For the young queen, her government and the whole political system were acutely vulnerable to heavy pressures from abroad and severe strain at home. From abroad the danger seemed the greatest for, as the queen ascended the throne, England was still in a state of war.

Today the English traveller, driving south from Calais through the dull, flat countryside, hastens through the new town of Le Cateau with scarcely a thought about its historic past. But in 1559 all Europe waited on its deliberations: for here at Cateau-Cambrésis were gathered the eminent representatives of France, Spain and England, striving through the long months of negotiations, suspicion, threat, intrigue to restore peace after half a century of bloody warfare and tragic waste. Peace came at last in the spring of 1559. Bourbon and Hapsburg shook hands. But the men who made peace did not love peace. For them peace was no more than an interval between one act of aggression and the next. They made peace because they were exhausted, impoverished, troubled by domestic dissent. They delimited their frontiers: and England, the weakest of the three parties, was forced to yield up Calais and withdraw across the channel. For the first time since the Norman Conquest, five centuries earlier, the English channel was her southern frontier. Beyond that she held nothing. English monarchs continued to describe themselves until 1801 as kings and queens of France, but their tenuous rule over its territories ended for ever in the year 1559. Thereafter Englishmen came as either soldiers or guests, never as governors.

It was as well. Calais had lost most of its importance in the English wool trade; and militarily it would have been impossible to defend and supply. All this was known to Elizabeth and her ministers, but they retained a formal claim to the town; and the unfortunate Thomas Smith was sent on a special embassy in 1567, in keeping with a clause in the Treaty of Cateau-Cambrésis, to present himself at the French Court and to demand its return. The demand was received by the Regent, Catharine de Medici, with bored contempt. It was the end of a long dominion.

The German Hapsburgs needed peace because they had been fighting not only the French and Turks abroad but the Lutherans at home. The Bourbons needed peace to deal with the Protestant dangers and social discord at home, which soon flared up into a series of civil wars. Nor could anyone foretell that England would long remain immune to the infection of civil war, an infection grown feverish in the ardour of religious passion. It was fortunate for the Elizabethan nation that, though the passion burned intensely in some Englishmen, there were many more whose faith, like that of their queen, was incombustible. But the outlook in 1559 seemed worse for England than for her continental neighbours.

Many Englishmen, like Sir Henry Killigrew, who was present during the treaty negotiations, believed that it contained a secret clause between France and Spain committing them to root out Protestantism wherever it might survive. If this belief arose from vague expressions of an ideological common policy by Hapsburg and Bourbon, it derived also from too superficial a view of the diplomatic relations between the great powers of Europe. Philip ii, the King of Spain, whose Catholicism was said to be of the most impeccable and fervent kind, had somehow to combine his Catholicism with the imperial office of King of Spain. If Protestantism in England were destroyed, and the only way to do so was to destroy the queen and her government, then the successor to the throne would almost certainly be Mary, Queen of Scots, who was also briefly Queen of France and under the high patronage of the French House of Guise. To destroy Protestantism in England would be to lengthen and strengthen the hold of France in the British Isles and thereby undo the uneasy balance of power accomplished in 1559. Philip ii would find himself in a worse position than at the end of the war. Hence Elizabeth must be shielded against those who would overthrow her. To Philip it seemed that the best thing for him to do would be to marry Elizabeth herself who, if she could accept Philip ii, could certainly accept Catholicism. But Elizabeth could not accept Philip ii; yet still she must be preserved. As a result the rejected suitor found himself in the ambiguous role of the Catholic protector of an illegitimate Protestant queen. Such were the political realities of the time. So if we remember Elizabeth as a saviour of Protestantism in England, we should not forget Philip ii.

The returning Protestant exiles did not forget Philip ii. For he had been the husband of Mary Tudor and shared with her, unfairly, the obloquy of persecution during the second half of her short reign. And many of these exiles returned eager for vengeance and resolved never to have to go on their travels again. To them the solution to the current problems was simple enough: let the Anglican church be purified of its Catholic relics so that it could attract all men of the true faith and guard itself against any repetition of the Marian episode; let the queen purify herself of any hope of compromise with the Catholics; and let her marry a staunch Protestant and propagate a dynasty which would defend the faith.

Such, in short, was the aim of these men of pure and exclusive faith. Puritans they therefore came to be called: not because they were pure in their way of life – some of their highest patrons had the lowest morals – but because they thought that they could purify the church. They had orderly minds: they wanted an ordered church, disciplined, logically organised, of precise doctrine and exclusive membership. They wanted the Church of England to be a closed shop. They could understand what Calvin stood for – who reading his *Institutes* could not? – but they had the darkest suspicions as to where the queen stood. They were quite clear that here was no general to lead them forward to annihilate the enemy.

Again these contemporaries oversimplified the situation. Here was no clear cut conflict between black and white, good and evil. Men like the diplomat, Sir Henry Killigrew, who believed that there was an unbridgeable chasm between the two faiths contributed towards its making. But for many people, including the queen, the division was not final or complete. Where faith divided, she believed, political interest and patriotism could still unite. So could music. William Byrd, the madrigalist was a life-long Catholic, but this did not prevent his becoming organist of the Chapel Royal. John Dowland, another fine composer, was less fortunate in the royal favour, perhaps because he had been a renegade Protestant. But Lady Petre, a staunch Catholic in Essex, enjoyed the special protection of the queen; while another Catholic, the Earl of Worcester, became her Master of the Horse. (The oft-repeated story that Lord

Howard of Effingham, the commander of the English forces against the Armada, was a Catholic has no basis in fact.)

As time passed the old memories of persecution faded, and some of the fears proved groundless. Protestants and Catholics found it possible to live together and to stand together in face of national danger. But it was impossible to foresee in 1599 what the position would be in 1599. The more forceful of the Protestant parliamentarians refused to be fed on the queen's hopes. They wanted an English church which was narrowly partisan in its faith and practices. But the queen resisted. We know now that the Anglican Settlement of 1559 was no carefully conceived, broad settlement skilfully designed to embrace diverse opinion. It was the result of a struggle and it was the compromise of pressure, pressure to which the queen had been forced to yield.

The Elizabethan Church Settlement was then, in some respects, a ramshackle affair, with its curious combination of traditional Catholic practice with new Protestant doctrine, of old Catholic hierarchy (with the exception of Pope, cardinal and abbot) but with a secular prince as its head. To the puritans, the great statutes of 1559, which re-founded the Church of England, were inadequate for the situation. The Act of Supremacy was too gentle with Catholics, in merely excluding them from office. The Act of Uniformity established a church which had too much in it of the church of Mary and too little of the church of Geneva. If it placed the Catholic clergy under heavy restraint, it was lenient – so the critics thought – to the layman in that he was merely fined one shilling a week for not attending the parish church.

This whole framework was peculiarly English, and peculiarly English it remained. It found its own preachers, administrators and philosophers of whom John Jewell, Archbishop Matthew Parker and Richard

Hooker were but three among many. Because it was a compromise it was under continuous and heavy fire. But, in spite of what its critics said, it did uphold Protestantism in England and brought hope to Protestantism in Europe. In a time of rapid dissolution and fundamental change it is always something of an achievement to survive. The Church of England survived.

J. A. Froude, the historian, writing in the middle of the nineteenth century, said that by the Church of the Reformation he meant the church 'of private judgment, of an open Bible, of lay independence of bishop or priest'. From his other writings it is clear that he meant also national independence; and these too are the things that Anglicanism meant to contemporaries. Elizabethan Anglicanism was a frame of mind. It is possible, on theological grounds, to criticise the inconsistencies within official doctrine. It may be that, if the settlement had contained less of the old order in the shape of bishops, archdeacons, deans, and less of the traditional ritual, it might have been spared some of the stresses of the seventeenth and later centuries. But it would have sacrificed also much of its inherent English culture and its sense of an ordered society. That sense of order stood it in good stead amid the social and religious convulsions which lay ahead for western Europe.

The decisions as to the future of the English church – and perhaps also of English society – were taken in the space of a single decade, roughly from 1559 until 1569. But again we emphasise that much more than religion was involved. It is well known, for example, that the local lord, knight or esquire, tended to set the pattern of his district, as he had always done in the medieval past. Thus, when we look for the distribution of Catholicism in Essex, we find pockets of Catholics in many cases concentrated near some dominant family of the same faith, such as the Petres or the Wisemans. This is merely one of numerous examples to remind us that the political, social and cultural framework of Elizabethan England was dominated by patronage from top to bottom, from the crown to the peasantry. When Father Gerrard, the missionary priest, came back to England in the 1590s, he concentrated on the country houses. This was not because he was a snob, as has been alleged, but because he knew where the roots of influence were to be found. If we try to explain the political and religious divisions in terms of politics and religion alone we miss their essentials, the close personal, social, historic links which joined a group together in the vague bonds of patronage.

We may take as our example the Rising of the Northern Earls of 1569. We know that in the northern counties of England much of the old faith survived and that, in 1569, men took to arms to re-establish the Catholic religion by force. It was the last time in English history that such an attempt had any remote chance of success. Of the religious sincerity of many of the men involved there can be no question. But much else was involved as well. The leaders of the rebellion, Charles Neville, 6th Earl of Westmorland and Thomas Percy, 7th Earl of Northumberland, if they clung to the old faith, represented also an older social order, the aristocratic domination of the shires. That order was being deliberately undermined by the Tudors. To the Tudors this ancient authority of the great secular lord was a menace to the centralised authority of the crown. Nor were they prepared to allow these barons as of right to serve on their council, as they might claim by long out-dated feudal custom. The Tudors wanted ministers of their own choosing, answerable to themselves alone.

Blocked in their ambition to rule, some of these noblemen had withdrawn to their own shires where they ruled as princes, impervious to the thunderbolts directed at them by the central government in London.

If they could not rule at the centre, they would ignore the centre and rule at home. But these centrifugal tendencies were no less intolerable to the crown, even though it was often unable to do much about it. Such a state of unstable equilibrium could not last indefinitely. In France during this period it culminated in a devastating series of civil wars. In England it led to the Northern Rebellion. Like their predecessors in the Pilgrimage of Grace more than a generation before, the rebels affirmed their loyalty to the crown but swore to remove the evil, upstart ministers who were destroying the great traditions of English society and government; this time it was men like the Cecils and the Dudleys. But the future lay with the Cecils and the Dudleys not the Percies and the Nevilles. These noble families survived; but the broken peasantry in full retreat in the north country symbolised that the old feudal order was passing away.

The old order was linked with the old faith in so intimate and complex a manner that it is impossible to disentangle the one from the other. Yet the very survival of Catholicism in this country depended upon its not being closely identified either with a dying order of society or with rebellion. It must somehow identify itself – as it had done by the end of the century – with the national interest (especially in a time of danger), irrespective of its religious complexion. These indeed were the sentiments of many Catholics; but their efforts to associate themselves with the existing political order received a major setback with the issue of the papal Bull of excommunication and deposition against the queen in 1570. It came too late to help the rebels, too late to depose the queen; but soon enough to strengthen and appear to justify those favouring a ruthless policy of extermination against the Catholics. These zealots overrated the power of the Bull. They forgot that Rome was a thousand miles from London and that this island, far away on the northwest frontier of Christendom, had more than once in the past heard papal injunctions which it had declined to obey. Once again in 1570 the English Catholics declined to obey. But it took them a whole generation to cancel in the public mind the association of English Catholicism with the Bull and both with rebellion. Only when the Spanish Armada had been met and defeated without a single hostile move against the government by English Catholics and a good deal which pointed in the opposite direction, only then at last in the governing classes did there evolve a recognition that Catholics could be as loyally the queen's subjects as were Protestants.

This does not mean that any movement for Catholic toleration developed in England. The notion of official toleration for religious diversity was completely out of keeping with the sixteenth century outlook. Indeed, in the 1570s when the missionary priests coming back to England launched a powerful campaign of propaganda and conversion, official persecution intensified. In 1581 the fine for non-attendance at church was raised savagely to £20 a week; and, in 1585, simply to be a priest in England meant sentence of death for treason. Yet there was a great disparity between the passing of a statute and its enforcement. The queen certainly, and a few of her ministers also, while punishing the extremists barbarously – as well as some of the noblest spirits of the age – worked for a *détente* with the moderates. The whole situation is, of course, meaningless if we try to judge it in the light of our present attitudes to matters of faith. In the 1580s the situation was profoundly different. The English governing classes felt that they were members of a nation in peril of extinction and they struck, in fear no less than in hatred, at the noncon-formist sector of their society, which they felt to be a channel for foreign command. All that can be said – and it is not saying much – is that Catholics were treated better in England than were Protestants in Spain or Jews in most countries of Europe.

But nothing should obscure the fact that the Elizabethan government was a persecuting and intolerant government. Some of its members would have used every resource to eliminate the Catholic leadership – and more especially its alternative monarch Mary, Queen of Scots. For the Scottish queen, driven from her own country in 1568 after a series of intrigues culminating in the murder of her husband and her marriage to his murderer, was now an exile in England. Worse still she was the magnet for one plot after another directed against Elizabeth. Even so, to the call for political bloodshed Elizabeth turned a deaf ear. But all alike looked forward to the end of Roman Catholicism in England.

And yet, if an Englishman of the fifteenth century could come back in the twentieth and attend a service at, for example, Westminster Abbey or York Minster, or indeed in almost any parish church, he would see much that was familiar. He would, of course, be surprised to find that the service was now conducted in English, and that the taking of communion had assumed a different character. But the service would in many respects be unchanged; so would the vestments of the clergy; so would the internal appearance of the church with its altar, pulpit, choir, with its elaborate tombs, its effigies and stained glass windows.

If he went further afield to Yorkshire, he would come upon Fountains Abbey, still lovely though a ruin, and he would discover that there and elsewhere a whole order of society, monks, nuns and friars, had in the sixteenth century been cut out of English society; and on enquiry he would learn much else. But in many respects he would find a church still tenacious of its ancient ways. Archbishop Laud who, in the seventeenth century, claimed that the Anglican Church was the ancient

English church – not a church created by the Reformation – has, at least in this, been vindicated.

Yet, supposing we merely cross to Holland and imagine, for example, a Dutchman, returning after five centuries to worship in the Cathedral in Utrecht? There indeed he would be conscious of profound change. He would notice the bare, undecorated cathedral; the broken monuments still showing their wounds and conveying, after so long, the religious fury which burst on the Netherlands; the simple Calvinist service; the synodal form of church organisation, with the old hierarchy completely swept away. He would at once see with his own eyes that his countrymen of the sixteenth century wrought a revolution which left its permanent mark on the thought and culture of the Dutch people.

But what would have happened if our fifteenth-century Englishman, unwilling to wait until the twentieth century, had come back in the reign of Elizabeth I? And supposing he had not gone to church but had travelled through the English shires and looked at the secular buildings? Then surely he would have noticed the clear marks of change. If the monasteries had gone, many castles still stood; but the English aristocracy was changing its habits. Medieval noblemen had needed castles to defend themselves against each other, and often against the king. But by now, private war – other than skirmishes among neighbours – had disappeared. War against the crown was the most desperate gamble. The Tudor nobles could not hope to become the king's rivals, and many were the king's dependants: they owed their power to him and held it only by the king's consent and during the king's pleasure. On the day that Henry VIII withdrew his favour from Thomas Cromwell, his most powerful minister, Cromwell fell. No castle could avail these men if the royal patronage was withdrawn.

So when they built, they built for comfort. If an Elizabethan nobleman's houses needed to be big, it was not for defence against the queen but to be in a position to entertain her. (And to entertain her meant to entertain a vast retinue of her courtiers and servants, to feed their horses, accommodate their cartloads of baggage. The mind boggles at the logistics of an Elizabethan progress, in such times and on such roads.) Here was one reason – at least the ostensible one – for building the great new palaces at Longleat, Burghley, Holdenby, Theobalds.

This, of course, was prestige building; and it was based upon a powerful tradition. A nobleman had to live splendidly; not to do so showed him unworthy of his rank. Lord Burghley went out of his way to proclaim that he wished to live humbly and build moderately. No one believed him; and, in any case, his own description of that massive pile at Burghley is a complete travesty of the facts. Ostentation was an essential sign of rank – and prestige living was followed by prestige dying. The Marquess of Northampton lay unburied for weeks while frantic efforts were made to raise money to give him a funeral appropriate to so elevated a nobleman.

In these formative years of the Elizabethan age, English builders looked to Italian patterns, but they looked also to their own tastes and needs in comfort and light. Later on Francis Bacon bitterly complained that 'You shall have sometimes fair houses so full of glass that one cannot tell where to become to be out of the sun or cold.' Yet it was glass that the Elizabethans wanted. There developed a flourishing glass industry in England, although the better quality came from Normandy and the Low Countries. The contemporary remark that Hardwick Hall was 'more glass than wall' has a modern ring about it.

Nor were comfort and distinction the perquisites of the aristocracy alone. Losely, built in Surrey in the 1560s, like Chastleton, built at the end of the reign in Oxford-shire, reflect the ambition of the gentry; while Caius

College, Cambridge, reminds us of the great shift in building interest from the church to secular education. (Professor W. K. Jordan, in another context, has shown the vast swing in interest and endowment from religious purposes to secular charities in which education played so large a part.) If the city merchants and the yeomanry built less ostentatiously, they showed none the less a keen and strong sense of order and comfort.

Order was indeed very much in the contemporary mind. Men sought order in their building, order in the church, order in their social life. The great Statute of Artificers of 1563, which controlled labour conditions over a large field, has been the subject of controversy among historians for nearly a century. Was it simply designed to keep the poor in their place, as no more than a reservoir of cheap and plentiful labour, especially for agriculture? Or was it a method of maintaining good conditions of life and work for all Englishmen? Was it a primitive example of capitalist exploitation or did it offer the first glimpses of state planning? This can provide an absorbing academic debate; but the Elizabethans would not have seen the point of it. For them it was one of many attempts to maintain some degree of social order, a way of continuing along national lines what the church and the gilds had achieved – or were believed to have achieved – on a local basis.

Long afterwards, in the last decade of the century, Richard Hooker would put this dream of order into words, in a passage in his *Ecclesiastical Polity*. 'I am not ignorant', he wrote, 'that by Law Eternal the learned for the most part do understand the order, not which God hath eternally purposed himself in all his works to observe, but rather that which, with himself, he hath set down as expedient to be kept by all his creatures, according to the several condition wherewith he hath indued them.' Of this divine order, natural law was a part: and natural law is based on the regular relations between all the elements of nature, that is, order. What would happen, Hooker asks:

if the Prince of the Lights of Heaven, which now as a giant doth run his unwearied course, should as it were through a languishing faintness begin to stand and rest himself; if the Moon should wander from her beaten way, the times and seasons of the year blend themselves by disordered and confused mixture, the Winds breathe out their last gasp, the Clouds yield no rain, the Earth be defeated of Heavenly influence, the Fruits of the Earth pine away as children at the withered breasts of their Mother, no longer able to yield them relief? What would become of Man himself whom these things now do all serve?

Nature obeys order, he argues, and so must man.

The desire for order is strongest in a society which is in process of rapid change; and, by a paradox, it is strongest among those who have risen highest and most rapidly in a changing world. For, especially in the middle years of a man's life, he clings fast to the things and to the world he has made. The middle aged are conservative in a way in which the young and the old never are. The middle-aged men who sat in Parliament, and the middle-aged men who dominated the queen's council, had, by 1570, come far on the road to stability and perhaps even prosperity. These men were building sturdy houses, they were buying good furniture, collecting pictures, accumulating silver and plate; they were enjoying their parks, their gardens and orchards and the broad acres on which they grew corn or pastured sheep. They were reasonably contented with their lot. It was a mood shared by the great conservative sitting on the throne of England. They had had enough of revolution and experiment, and they stirred uneasily at the renewed signs of change.

III

Neither Peace nor War

1570-85

There are only two inevitable things in history. One is that night follows day; the other is that men die. All the rest are mere possibilities. It is all too easy for historians wise after the event, to see war as inevitable. This is especially easy in the later Elizabethan period where everything seems to have advanced inexorably towards the grand climax of Armada year. To contemporaries nothing was inevitable. All that they could see in the middle years of the reign was an uneasy balance of possibilities. The heavy and continuous task of the government was to find some escape from this twilight situation without, on the one hand, sacrificing the national interest, or, on the other, advancing headlong into a catastrophic war.

To Elizabeth herself war was anything but inevitable. Throughout these fifteen years between the Bull of deposition in 1570 and the actual outbreak of war with Spain in 1585, she used every conceivable device to reduce the temper of the times. But optimist – or procrastinator – as she was, she remained sensitive to the sudden emergence of grave peril. An amusing example of the widespread feeling of insecurity occurred shortly after the issue of the Bull of deposition.

Philip II, already three-times widowed, had negotiated a match between himself and Anne of Austria, daughter of the Emperor Maximilian II. All that remained in 1570 was to convey the lady by sea from the

Netherlands to Spain. The Spanish commander, the Duke of Alva, decided to provide an escort appropriate to a future Queen of Spain, and appropriate also to defend so precious a cargo against the rebels and pirates infesting the seas. For rebels and pirates Elizabeth herself had little sympathy, whatever their nationality. But who could tell what other instructions the commander of the escort fleet carried with him as he sailed up the English channel? There existed a very real anxiety that a large part of this Spanish navy might be detached for an assault on England in fulfilment of the Bull. What better wedding present could His Most Catholic Majesty offer his bride than the news that the greatest Protestant threat to the Faith had been removed? Against so real a danger some provision had to be made. So, although Elizabeth had not been invited to the wedding, she felt that she could not afford to be absent from the preliminaries. She accordingly mobilised the fleet. With due decorum it too stood guard over the royal bride. All went well. Thus an Austrian princess, on her way to her marriage, was seen safely up the channel by two powerful navies, one Catholic and the other, at a watchful distance, Protestant. They did not exchange a single shot.

Not all incidents ended so harmoniously. And throughout the period Spain was as much concerned as England with what happened in the channel ports. For if England was still at peace, Spain was at war, disastrously involved in a war in the Netherlands which was to last on into the seventeenth century. A series of judicious marriages by his Hapsburg ancestors, vastly enlarging their territories, had made the Netherlands part of Philip II's empire; the most industrious, the most prosperous and now the most rebellious part of his empire. The situation was immensely complex and it is not to be explained simply in terms of religion. Many of his Netherlands subjects were as Catholic as the king.

Many of their descendants, still Catholic, live on in the modern state of Belgium, the successor of the southern Netherlands which in the end broke with the northern provinces and remained loyal to Spain. But, for a time at least, these seventeen provinces of the north and south stood united in open rebellion against Spanish tyranny, a tyranny which to them spelled out heavy taxation, the suppression of local rights and the dark threat of the Inquisition. In the Calvinistic northern Netherlands resistance was fiercest, led by the warrior-statesman, William the Silent, and the movement pressed on towards full independence.

The story of this heroic endurance belongs to the history of European freedom; but in the late 1570s it was more acutely relevant to England's own prospect of survival. As far as Elizabeth was concerned, the best thing that the Dutch rebels could do would be to come to terms with Philip II. She assumed always that, in peace, his control would be somewhat remote and he would ultimately revert to the policy of his father, the Emperor Charles V, in devolving authority upon the Dutch themselves. On the other hand, while rebellion lasted, Philip would have to keep a large army in the Netherlands; and such a concentration of military power so near to the south coast of England meant that others besides the Dutch were in danger. In Elizabeth's eyes distance lent enchantment to the view. She preferred a Philip II away in Madrid to a Duke of Alva, his ruthless general, so uncomfortably close at hand.

The Dutch were less selective. They would submit to neither Philip II in Madrid nor to Alva in the Netherlands. They had reached the point of no return. They were determined to fight on to the end: first in their homeland: and then, when they were driven out, they fought in the channel, sailing into English ports when they had nowhere else to go. From now on in this sphere Elizabeth began to lose what little freedom of manoeuvre she had hitherto possessed. She could not let the Dutch be annihilated. Political opinion in England would not have stood by and seen a gallant Protestant people simply wiped off the map. Elizabeth's reasons were not ideological: she preferred religion and diplomacy to be kept in separate categories. But if the Dutch fell, then the Spanish army of occupation would stay on, ever ready to be occupied in another mission. If the Dutch held out, but without English help, then they would sooner or later turn to the French, who might come as friends but stay as rulers. In that case the Dutch – and Elizabeth – would have leapt out of the Spanish frying pan into the French fire. Elizabeth's hope that the Dutch might gain a kind of dominion status under Spain, with England acting as honest broker to both sides, proved illusory. In the end she had to intervene to save the Netherlands from both Spain and France. But as ever she was unwilling to commit large sums of money and large armies of men to a war in which, at least superficially, England was not directly involved. Quantitatively her half-hearted help was small in this phase. But she gave the Dutch their most precious asset, time. Given time, they forged the mood and the means for complete national independence.

Until about the end of this period of fifteen years there was an English ambassador in Madrid and a Spanish ambassador in London. The two countries were at peace. But as an Elizabethan, the diplomat Sir Henry Wotton, recorded in the next century, an ambassador was a man sent to lie abroad for the benefit of his country. Lying was probably the least of his vices. Ambassadors were often expected to maintain an elaborate espionage service and to establish close contact with the forces of resistance to the very government to which they were accredited. English ambassadors did it abroad; foreign ambassadors did the same thing in London.

At this time the Spanish ambassador in London, de

Spes, was the centre of a complicated intrigue. But in order to understand the rôle he was playing it is necessary to look back briefly to the arrival of his predecessor, de Silva – an abler man than he, who had come to London in 1564. That the government in Madrid had assigned a special task to its London embassy is clear enough.

'At the first interview with the queen,' ran the ambassador's instructions from his king, 'you will not introduce business at all but simply deliver my letter of credence to her and visit her in my name, complimenting her with the fairest words you can use.' The ambassador was to assure the queen that he had orders 'to endeavour to please her in all things', that his policy would be directed towards the maintenance of 'our mutual alliance' and that 'nothing will be wanting on our part to this end'. He also carried other instructions, not for the ear of the queen. 'Many of the English people,' he was reminded, 'are depraved and have abandoned our holy and only true ancient Catholic religion'; but others had remained faithful. These Catholic dissenters 'should be encouraged and supported, and I enjoin you to do this whenever you can, and at the same time to endeavour to keep them in the good will and devotion which, I understand, they display towards us', – that is to the King of Spain. 'This however must be done with such secrecy, dissimulation and dexterity as to give no cause for suspicion to the queen or her advisers, as it is evident that much evil might follow if the contrary were the case.' There were also other small services which the ambassador was to render, such as 'obtain information with diligence as to the Spanish heretics who may be there, their names, what part of Spain they come from and their rank', and he was to forward the information to the King of Spain and to the inquisitor-general.

De Silva reached England in June 1564, and was granted an audience of the queen on the 22nd. The Court was at Richmond and there he found the queen ready to play her full part in the diplomatic charade. In the presence chamber where she received him, the queen was 'listening to a keyed instrument that was being played, and as soon as she saw me took three or four steps towards me and embraced me'. She spoke to him in Italian since, as she said, she was not sure which language to use. He answered in Latin, handing her his letter of credence. She read it, replied to the ambassador very warmly in Latin 'with elegance, facility and ease', and enquired very tenderly after the health of the king and his family. She then raised one or two political questions but the ambassador, acting on his instructions, asked that these matters be left to a separate occasion since now he wanted to hear only of her 'friendship and affection', for the Spanish king. He said too that on another occasion he would tell her of the kindliness and brotherhood' that the king felt for her, as did Spaniards in general; a feeling, he added, that was unfortunately not reciprocated by all the queen's subjects. With these formal exchanges over, the queen withdrew, having embraced the ambassador once more, and he now settled down to the routine business of political intrigue to oust her principal minister, William Cecil, from office.

De Silva was a subtle diplomat who knew just how far he could go. De Spes, who had succeeded him in 1568, was a clumsy intriguer who was prepared to believe everything – at least everything told him by Ridolfi, an Italian financier working in London. Ridolfi claimed to know of a deep, widespread yearning in England for the overthrow of Elizabeth and her government, to be followed by the accession of Mary, Queen of Scots, who was to be married to the Duke of Norfolk. Such knowledge as Ridolfi believed he had about England was matched by the knowledge that the English counter-espionage service had about him and his activities. The tangled web of the Ridolfi Plot caught and destroyed the vacillating Duke of Norfolk in 1572. It caught and destroyed Mary, Queen of Scots, as well; but it took another fifteen years for the axe to fall. To many of the parliamentarians it was a long, unnecessary and dangerous delay. For Mary was the focal centre of an unsleeping opposition to the Elizabethan government, but an opposition from which responsible Catholic opinion held entirely aloof.

The danger, however, lay not in responsible Catholic opinion, as subsequent events clearly showed, but in a few young firebrands and a few maladjusted men of more advanced years. That is a danger which besets rulers at any time. The assassin's dagger – or gun – is much more often held by a paranoiac than by a politician. And from that danger Elizabeth was never for one moment free until the end of her days. Yet if Mary was the inspiration of the opposition and therefore the prisoner of Elizabeth, she was also her *protégé*.

All this enables us to see another facet of Elizabeth's mind and temperament. Her ministers lamented what they regarded as a permanent weakness in her character: the use of procrastination as an instrument of policy. But when it came to shedding blood, it was more than procrastination. She had a profound detestation of killing however judicially it might be carried out. When the victim in this case was to be one who had been anointed Queen of France and Scotland, then the burden of decision became unbearable. It would have been possible at any time after 1572 to have formulated judicial grounds for a capital sentence on Mary, insecure though these grounds might be – and they were by no means secure even in 1587 when she was in fact executed. But from now onwards the political reasons for Mary's removal outdistanced the judicial argument. For while she lived, Elizabeth and the realm were in danger. Yet still Elizabeth, alone, stood between Mary and the political logic of events.

This policy seemed especially difficult to defend in the year 1572. For that year in France, at the moment of reconciliation between Catholic and Protestant on St Bartholomew's eve, saw the situation change overnight into a bloodbath of staggering dimensions: the righteous slaughter of Huguenots under the instigation of the Catholic Regent, Catharine de Medici. The exact causes and character of the Massacre have in them still something which is incomprehensible. But to English Protestants the events gave clear warning of what might happen in England if an assassin's deed, or foreign invasion, put Mary on the throne. Yet still Elizabeth maintained an evasive, yet stubborn, resistance to the urgent pressures of her statesmen. Hence another paradox: Mary's survival depended upon the survival of Elizabeth, whom Mary's supporters were pledged to destroy.

There were other gathering pressures upon Elizabeth. If she was being urged to bring direct help to the Dutch and therefore challenge Spain, she was also confronted by a Spanish threat on the high seas. Spain had, on papal authority and by means of a widely stretched army of occupation, gained an extensive and indefensible – in every sense of that word – overlordship in the New World across the Atlantic. What Spain did not hold, was held, on like authority, by Portugal. And since Portugal was annexed by Spain in 1580, Philip II was now master of enormous lands across the Atlantic as well as territories in Africa and elsewhere. This authority Elizabethan seamen declined to recognise.

Englishmen came as traders – often slave traders; and when they were refused free entry into American ports, they fought their way in. Sometimes too they spared themselves the full Atlantic crossing by detaining Spanish ships on their way back from America and diverting their treasures to places where they were much appreciated. Some of the silver and gold that the Spaniards had looted – or mined – ultimately found their way into the south coast ports of England and, in part, into the crown's possession. But we must not exaggerate either their quantity or their importance. For from that day until this a romantic and heroic aura has surrounded these exploits.

The heroism of men like Gilbert, Hawkins and Drake is beyond question and beyond praise. But when a reckoning has been taken of the profits and loss on piracy and privateering, it is doubtful whether they yielded a net gain. They were bad for trade; but these Atlantic seamen felt that they had no alternative since the Spaniards prohibited their trade with the New World. None the less, these activities diverted a lot of manpower and shipping to the speculative gains of loot. And these limited prospects of profit declined when, in the 1590s, the Spaniards fortified strategic points in America and learned also to beat off the attacks at sea. The economic and social tragedy in all this is that both England and Spain engaged their finest minds and bravest men in the deadly task of destruction. So did the French and Dutch. But it was not all loss. The second half of the sixteenth century saw the opening of a new phase in maritime history which shifted the balance of power of the whole world. Out of the experience gained in both eastern and western oceans, the three maritime nations of north-western Europe, England, the Nether-lands and France entered, in the seventeenth century, upon an age of unparalleled growth. It became an age also of enormous military commitments as imperial war-fare spread to all the known continents.

All this could but obscurely be foreseen. And in the field of science, too, the frontiers of the new worlds could be no more clearly perceived. If the literature, the politics, the religion show many signs of the effects of humanism, to which we have referred in an earlier chapter, it is much more difficult to determine what influence science was exerting upon the Elizabethan way of life. If we define science as the knowledge of nature acquired by free investigation, that is to say, by enquiry which is free from dogma, then the influence of science was negligible. Men were not free. The weight of tradition – by no means only religious tradition – lay heavily on all branches of enquiry. Even the leading men of the age did not possess either the intellectual equipment or the physical resources to attempt original analyses in the realm of nature. Many of the investigations drifted uncertainly between a disciplined, rational examination of the material world and pure charlatanry. Science and magic were practised side by side, and sometimes by the same man, well exemplified in the celebrated Dr John Dee, mathematician, astronomer, geographer, astrologer, magician. As when we watch Shakespeare's *Midsummer Night's Dream* or *The Tempest*, we hover uncertainly between two worlds.

The sixteenth century in England was not an age of science, nor was it an age of science anywhere in Europe. It is true that Copernicus had issued his *De Revolutionibus Orbium Coelestium* in 1543 and had posited therein a sun-centred universe, not the classic and Christian one in which all things revolved round the earth. But it needed three more generations and the work of Galileo to make this discovery the great challenge it became to the basic concepts of religion and philosophy. Some men, including Englishmen like John Dee and Thomas Digges, responded actively to the work of Copernicus; but to the majority of scholars it was, in the sixteenth century, no more than an hypothesis which could not be proved.

Meanwhile, in medicine, another revolution was in the making. In 1543, in the same year as the appearance of Copernicus's work, Vesalius issued his *De Humani*

A Tudor Law court in session: the Court of Wards and
Liveries with Sir William Cecil, Lord Burghley, as presiding
judge. By an unknown artist. Engraved in the eighteenth
century by Vertue.

William Cecil, later Lord Burghley, Secretary of State 1558–72, Master of the Queen's Wards 1561–98, Lord Treasurer 1572–98. Artist unknown.

Left: Queen Elizabeth I presiding at the opening of Parliament in November 1584. The ceremony is taking place in the House of Lords, as it still does, with the Members of the House of Commons standing at the Bar. From an engraving by Thomas Glover.

The tomb of Robert Cecil, Earl of Salisbury, in Hatfield parish church, close to Hatfield House, which he built. The upper effigy shows him in the full robes of the Lord Treasurer, holding his staff of office, while below is represented the bare skeleton of mortal man.

Right: The draft preamble to the subsidy bill of 1566 with Queen Elizabeth's angry comment at the foot in her own handwriting. She strongly objected to her promise to declare the succession being incorporated in a statute. Hence 'I know no reason why any my private answers to the realm should serve for prologue to a subsidies-book'. But she never in fact 'declared the succession'.

Therwith we cannot but also thankfully remember to yor maiestie that it hathe pleased the same to signifye vnto vs that yow did not in respecte of yor owne desyre in this behalf to haue the Successor of the Crowne declared, for that anyone myght conceaue the same of desyre to procede from vs (as indede it did) of more dutye and loue towardes yor highnes yor realmes and countreis and not of any other disposytyon or pryuate purpose. And seinge it is suche of yor owne disposytyon and naturall loue towardes vs to be yor comforte that rather than yor realme shuld therefore runne in lacke of a Successor or of settled almyghtye god wold shewe of yor owne goodnes in due tyme after yor mariage yow wold by goddes helpe thewes at god apperyshme perell to yor good (god defende) declare the Successor In whose consentinge tyme aboue yor owne hadinge of yor promise and assent of yor realme shall thinke most mete in whose goodnes in whose youghte thereof accordinge to law and iustice ought to be vttered and remayne to the youfull comforte of vs all And so humyne pryyma that faire thankes to the same in the forefront of yor small but a most wyse and wyllynge trust theirof most humble rommynstion, we do likewyse beseche yor ma^{tie} to receaue the wyll that plenteth as or firste of yor faythfulnes, and render, we hath so bare to yor ma^{tie}, and that it may be reuerted in some plenewye.

[cipher line]
[cipher line]

but this two concernyngs into one meaning and my counsell as all giuen let not offer regard them selues so holy as I haue no counsell left for me let them knowe that I knewe those I folowed not, that some of them wold my poure councels better serued me that Her shrewde practises could annulli with me I knewe no reason whi ourr my answere to the realme shuld bene for profit to a subsidies bere neither

The Spanish Armada in crescent formation, with the English fleet coming out of Plymouth behind them. Engraving by John Pine. House of Lords tapestry, now destroyed.

Top right: The Protestant Succession; a picture *c.* 1570.

Bottom right: The Somerset House Peace Conference ending the long war with Spain which had begun in 1585. The English delegation is on the right, led by Sir Robert Cecil, the Secretary of State. By Marc Gheeraierdts, the Younger.

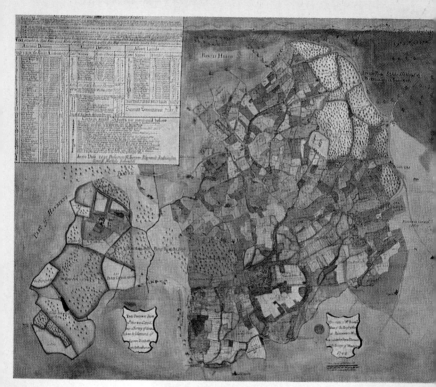

Top: Manorial map of Fakenham, Worcestershire, showing both open fields and enclosure. By John Blagrave, 1591.

Bottom: A Celestial Chart for 1590, by Thomas Hood; the earliest chart of the stars to be made by an Englishman.

Eliza Triumphans by William Rogers, in commemoration of the Victory of the Armada. The queen appears as Peace, with victory on one side and Plenty on the other offering her crowns.

The manner of there fishing.

An Elizabethan banquet and scenes in the life of Sir Henry Unton. Detail from a painting by an unknown artist.

Left: One of John White's pictures of the native Indian of North America.

Oak arm chair (early seventeenth century).

Tigerware jug, 1564

Oak coffer and
joint stool (late Elizabethan)

testum

porticus

sedilia

orchestra

ingressus

mimorum aedes

proscenium

Planeties siue arena.

Ex observationibus Londinensibus
Johannis de witt

View of the Thames at London Bridge, the only bridge over the river. From an engraving by C. J. Visscher (1616).

Left: Interior of the old Swan Theatre, based on a rough drawing by the traveller Johannes de Witt.

A preacher at old St Paul's Cross, a place sometimes used by the government for the dissemination of propaganda.

Corporis Fabrica which revolutionised the study of anatomy and therefore of medicine. Like Copernicus, Vesalius owed much to his predecessors; and like him he had to wait for his methods and conclusions to bear fruit. But both of them undermined the classic framework of established scientific doctrine that derived from Ptolemy the second-century astronomer and from Galen the second-century physician. Yet the original authorities had remarkable powers of survival. The Elizabethan President of the College of Physicians, Dr John Caius – re-founder of the Cambridge College which bears his name – imprisoned a young doctor who was said to have declared that Galen was sometimes in error. Some educated Elizabethans were, however, fully awake to the new processes in scientific thought; but it was not until the seventeenth century that Englishmen like William Harvey and Isaac Newton made major contributions to the advancement of science.

Elizabethans were alive also to such progress as was being made in Europe in the more practical branches of knowledge. England herself had neither the technical skill nor the financial resources to develop her mines, exploit her metals or manufacture her armaments. Hence there began the slow, expensive, painful process of attracting to England the finance and skill of the metallurgists from Augsburg and elsewhere, for example, the firms of Haug and Hoechstetter, prospecting for copper and calamine (the zinc ore) for the manufacture of brass. There were technical troubles, labour disputes, financial difficulties. In spite of government support to the Mines Royal and the Mineral and Battery Works, both granted royal patents in 1568, progress was slow, profits, if any, small. But lessons were learned, and a slow unsteady progress was evident, not only in metallurgy but in coal mining. Coal was coming in for both domestic and industrial use, but again only slowly. Technical problems and insuperable transport difficulties prevented any dramatic increase in its use. There was no radical change in the methods, material or organisation of industry. England held to her accustomed ways. The alleged industrial revolution of the sixteenth century can exist only in the eye of the beholder.

But in one sphere these years did see fundamental change and a development of major and permanent importance. In literature, England now began to gain an ascendancy in European culture which she has never lost. We can set no single date to these developments but from the late 1570s onwards it was evident that English literature had entered upon a great creative phase. It was not always so.

To Professor C. S. Lewis the middle years of the sixteenth century are the 'drab' years. Of the men of the time he writes: 'Their prose is clumsy, monotonous, garrulous; their verse either astonishingly tame and cold, or if it attempts to rise, the coarsest fustian. . . . Nothing is light, or tender, or fresh. All the authors write like elderly men.' He sees it as 'an earnest, heavy-handed, commonplace age'. This may be somewhat exaggerated. But anyone who has had to plough his joyless way through the *Mirror for Magistrates*, a long contemporary narrative in bad verse, knows how much contemporaries endured, and how much indeed is still endured in the cause of scholarship.

And then the change came. The most fascinating problem of the last three decades of the sixteenth century is not, how did England defeat the Armada, or what caused the new attitudes in Parliament and society, developments which can in some measure be explained, but what brought about that incredible efflorence of prose and poetry of unparalleled beauty, majesty and power?

We know of course that the social and political conditions of these years provided for playwrights and poets the immense stimuli to write and write well. There was a cultivated Court presided over by a queen very conscious of her rôle of literary patron and anxious to pose before Europe as herself a member of a brilliant literary movement. The great aristocrats like Leicester supported a company of actors, assured them of an appreciative audience and – more important – a means of livelihood. The London middle classes and the artisans did the same on the south bank of the Thames and elsewhere, providing in their way a livelihood for actors and playwrights, but providing also the pressures for a virile naturalism so characteristic of the Elizabethan theatre. The spread of secular education also played an important part. For the country gentleman no longer thought it enough if his solicitor or tutor or bishop could claim to be educated men. He himself went to the university or to one of the Inns of Court or spent successive periods in university and Inn. William Cecil and his son Robert went in turn to Cambridge and Gray's Inn, but there is no evidence of a degree or being called to the bar. Thousands of lesser men did the same thing. The dominant classes in town and country could read and write, could encourage and appreciate authors and poets. They found too in their works both the inspiration and justification for the expansionist aims of their economic and maritime enterprises.

Culture flourished where wealth accumulated. It is a fallacy to believe that the best poetry and prose are produced by bitter, impoverished and disappointed men. It is quite true that men of genius sometimes in their agony of mind yield up a masterpiece which could only derive from the depth and force of their grief and passion. But no one knows how many such men die with their best work unfinished and unknown. One of the reasons why men write is their desire to communicate a unique experience to their fellow men. Without an audience to appreciate and sustain them in this work, it is still possible for the best songs to go unsung. We sometimes forget that even poets die if they are without bread. The Elizabethans found an audience.

The second fallacy is that wealthy men and wealthy societies breed philistines. The evidence of ancient Greece is against it. So is the evidence of the Italian Renaissance. So is the evidence of the Elizabethan age. Some wealthy men are of course philistines; but so are some very poor ones. Philistinism gives no indication of a man's wealth but only of his lack of taste, sensitivity, education. And even a man devoid of sensitivity sometimes hopes that his name will outlast his possessions and be commemorated in the immortal work of one whose labours he has sustained. There is nothing in this argument to defend the gross inequalities in the distribution of wealth, which was so striking a feature of Elizabethan England; and there is much in this book which indicates the high price that ordinary men had to pay for the splendours of the governing classes. But if the historian is trying to explain the unparalleled phenomenon of late Elizabethan culture, he cannot ignore the fact that an acquisitive society is concerned with cultural no less than material acquisitions. That is how patronage – at its best – functions.

It does not follow from this that all the literature extolled the virtues of the existing social order. Some writers did indeed lavishly praise their patron or the queen; some described England as rather more than a 'demi-paradise' and have been taken a little too seriously by a number of historians of our own day. But there was also a significant literature of dissent. We may sometimes think of Edmund Spenser or Sir Walter Ralegh as court poets; but both of them were outspoken critics of the men in power. When, in 1590, Spenser published his *Faerie Queene*, it is true that he accompanied it with a dedication to Elizabeth I and with seventeen dedicatory sonnets to the statesmen and courtiers of the day, including Sir Christopher Hatton, William Cecil, Lord

Burghley, the Earl of Oxford, the Earl of Essex and Sir Walter Ralegh. But the poem itself reveals another side of the picture:

> The time was once, in my first prime years,
> When pride of youth forth pricked my desire,
> When I disdained amongst mine equal peers
> To follow sheep, and shepherds base attire.
> For further fortune then I would inquire
> And leaving home, to royal court I sought,
> Where I did sell myself for yearly hire,
> And in the Prince's garden daily wrought.
> There I beheld such vain-ness as I never thought.

We remember Spenser also for *The Ruines of Time* and for *Mother Hubberds Tale* with his fierce onslaught on the whole framework of court patronage. We remember Sir Walter Ralegh, too, in the same context, for his later poem *The Lie* is a massive attack on exactly the same system which, he says, is based on the corruption of a whole society:

> Tell men of high condition
> That manage the estate,
> Their purpose is ambition,
> Their practice only hate:
> And if they once reply,
> Then give them all the lie.

These are, of course, the words of men who failed; but it is none the less evidence that if the Court circle bred sycophants, it also bred critics who attacked the whole fabric of contemporary society. And where shall we find the most brief – and most powerful – condemnation of the false glamour of Elizabethan warfare? Nowhere better than in the work of that archetype of the romantic hero, Sir Philip Sidney's *Arcadia*, written in the 1580s. Of war he writes, 'for at the first, though it were terrible, yet Terror was decked so bravely with rich furniture, gilt swords, shining armours, pleasant pencils that the eye with delight had scarce leisure to be afraid'. So much for the glamour. His next sentence dissolves it all. 'But now all universally defiled with dust, blood, broken armours, mangled bodies, took away the mask and set forth Horror in his own horrible manner.'

But whether we turn again to their works for sheer pleasure or to use them as social documents of great and increasing value to the historian, we cannot for long be unconscious that we are in a world newly discovered by the Elizabethans, as promising and challenging as the El Dorado which they believed existed in the newly discovered world across the Atlantic.

The history of literature, by its very nature, can rarely have dates at which revolutions take place. It is concerned with phases, influences, trends, one stage merging with the next. And yet – one further extraordinary element in an already extraordinary story – these brief middling years of the reign do seem to mark almost dramatically an opening epoch.

For it was now in the early 80s that Spenser, having written *The Shephearde's Calendar*, had begun to write the *Faerie Queene*, the triumphant marriage of medieval allegorical poetry with the new Elizabethan concepts and setting. Thus perfecting a medieval poetic form, Spenser closed an age in English literature and pointed the way to a new exploration of the Elizabethan compromise of Christianity and humanism. Spenser is not the greatest of Elizabethan poets, but he is the first of them to write great and living verse firmly rooted in a medieval tradition. He is the first of them also to become a continuous influence upon modern English literature from Milton to Tennyson.

What Spenser was doing for verse, Richard Hooker and others would in due course do for prose to which pamphleteers like 'Martin Marprelate' and politicians like Peter Wentworth would add a fire of their own.

But it is Elizabethan verse which comes first to the mind when we think of these formative years; and it is well therefore to let Sir Philip Sidney, a master alike of prose and verse, speak his famous lines in *Apology for Poetry*. Of all the sciences, he tells us, the poet is monarch: 'For he doth not only show the way, but giveth so sweet a prospect into the way as will entice any man to enter into it. Nay, he doth, as if your journey should lie through a fair vineyard, at the very first give you a cluster of grapes that, full of that taste, you may long to pass further. . . . He cometh to you with words set in delightful proportion, either accompanied with, or prepared for, the well-enchanting skill of music; and with a tale, forsooth, he cometh unto you, with a tale which holdeth children from play, and old men from the chimney corner. . . .' *So sweet a prospect!* Not even Sidney, when he wrote these words, could have foreseen how dazzling a prospect was opening before the Elizabethans.

But these were the years without open warfare or secure peace. And now even the queen's most tenuous grasp upon peace was weakening. A few years after writing his *Apology*, Sidney was himself a soldier in the Netherlands where in 1586, as the result of a wound in battle, he died. His death is associated with a famous incident, often re-told in modern English. What follows is the story as it was first written down by an Elizabethan, his friend and biographer, Fulke Greville. Having been wounded, Sidney was

passing along by the rest of the army, where his uncle, the general [the Earl of Leicester], was; and being thirsty with excess of bleeding, he called for drink, which was presently brought him. But as he was putting the bottle to his mouth he saw a poor soldier carried along, who had eaten his last at the same feast, ghastly casting up his eyes at the bottle. Which Sir Philip perceiving, took it from his head before he drank, and delivered it to the poor man, with these words, 'Thy

71

necessity is yet greater than mine.' And when he had pledged this poor soldier, he was presently carried to Arnheim.

Like his friend whom he mourned, Greville was able to mingle the sweet with the bitter in the skilful texture of his style. It is hard to find a better example of the sophisticated simplicity of Elizabethan prose and of the whole Elizabethan way of life.

IV

The Darker Years

1585-1603

In 1585, when open war broke out with Spain, men felt bound together in a noble purpose: to defend the independence of their country and to fight in a larger European struggle, associated with patriotic Dutchmen and patriotic Frenchmen, against the obscurantist forces of evil, personified in Philip ii. Yet still Elizabeth tarried. 'I am sorry to see,' wrote Sir Francis Walsingham, the Secretary of State, to Lord Burghley, in June 1588, 'so great danger hanging over this realm, so slightly regarded and so carelessly provided for.' The Secretary of State was something of a fanatic – understandably, perhaps, for he had been an eye-witness of the Massacre of St Bartholomew's day in Paris. But many men would have acknowledged that there was some truth in what he said.

For Elizabeth, patriotism was not enough. After the heroism came the price: mounting debts, stagnant trade, unemployment, discontent, recrimination, war-weariness. And no one grew more weary of war than the queen. Perhaps we of this generation can understand something of what she felt. Anyone today who is over fifty has lived through two wars which, with an interval, lasted for eleven years altogether. The Elizabethans lived through a period of eighteen years of war with no interval. It is the longest period of continuous warfare in modern English history. Elizabeth was not alone in growing weary of the exhausting glory of a valiant cause. And as men grew weary of war, they grew weary also of the queen.

It was no wonder that she was criticised by contemporaries and that their criticisms were echoed by historians. Men said she gave too little for war and scattered what little she gave; that she counted every penny she lent and pressed her embattled allies to pay their debts; that she was ungrateful and ungracious to her generals at a time when her own strategic aims were fainthearted and confused.

It would indeed have been surprising if one who was in ultimate and unrelieved command of all the national effort, for so long a time of war, did not make mistakes. But it is true that a reluctant warrior fights under handicaps more debilitating than those which may afflict an eager soldier, born to war. Like Sir Robert Walpole a century and a half later, Elizabeth went to war hating it and hoping for peace. Why then did she go to war at all?

Primarily, this was because the governing assumptions of the preceding thirty years no longer prevailed. The balance of power between Spain and France – that is between rivals, which made impossible a major operation by either or both against England – was a balance which no longer held. France was weaker than Spain. By now the heir to the French throne was Henry of Navarre, a Protestant; and here was a situation which drove many French Catholics into a Spanish alliance. By now, too, William the Silent was dead, assassinated by a fanatic in 1584; and the annihilation of Dutch resistance seemed in sight. For the first time since her accession Elizabeth was faced with a gathering of hostile power which might deal out to the English the same fate that every moment awaited their Dutch allies. Now at last the implicit challenge from Spain became explicit. The queen acknowledged a state of open war. But, according to some, she proved unequal to

74

the occasion. 'If the late queen would have believed her men of war as she did her scribes,' wrote Sir Walter Ralegh, 'we had in her time beaten that great empire in pieces.' This is the view of a contemporary

It is not the view of Professor R. B. Wernham, our leading authority on Elizabethan diplomacy.[1] In a close analysis of her whole strategy in the war years, he has shown how her wide commitments, her central aim to keep the channel, and the channel ports, open and free, and her tragically slender financial resources permitted her to do what she did, but to do no more. At no time was she in a position, nor did she dare, to concentrate her forces to deliver a mortal blow at her enemy. (In essence she was in the position of England from 1941 to 1943, when the government was pressed to open a second front in Europe yet dared not reduce the home defences, for so large, aggressive and decisive a manoeuvre.) And even when the queen was at last keyed up for a dominant act, she found her commanders wanting. 'She was not one of England's great war leaders,' Professor Wenham concludes, 'and she only half achieved her aims. Yet to have helped the French monarchy to its feet, to have saved half the Netherlands from Spanish "tyranny", to have kept the other half out of French possession, and England itself out of bankruptcy, was a fair achievement against the Spain of Philip II.'

If Elizabeth was a reluctant warrior she was also a reluctant judge. Mary, Queen of Scots, her cousin, living now under the increasingly close confinement of the government, continued intermittently to be the centre of plots against the queen: not the instigator but the supporter. Many men judged her, in this, guilty of treason; and in 1585, by a special statute of Parliament provision was made that, on the next occasion, she

---

[1] R. B. Wernham, 'Elizabethan war aims and strategy' in *Elizabethan Government and Society*, ed. S. T. Bindoff *et. al.* (1961), pp. 340–368.

should be brought to trial and, if guilty, sentenced to death. The Babington Plot of 1586 provided the next occasion, and the skill of Sir Francis Walsingham ensured that it would not be missed. From that day to this controversy has raged as to how far she was guilty; and, in any case, if she was guilty, how far a foreign sovereign, who still claimed to be head of the Scottish state, could be made subject to English laws and an English Parliament. This legal issue and other doubts tormented Elizabeth herself; and during this paralysis of her will, Burghley and the other ministers virtually took the power of decision from her and forced her hand. In 1587 the executioner's axe at Fotheringay ended the problem but enlarged the controversy.

In a last letter to Spain Mary bequeathed her rights to the throne of England (which she did not possess) to Philip II (who was in no position to receive it). But if ever there was a favourable moment to claim and conquer England, it was now. The weakness of his French allies and his Dutch enemies alike pressed him to the belief that he was in the position to fight the last battle of a long war.

The war was fought on the seas, in the channel, in Spanish ports in the Old World and the New; it was fought in France and in the Netherlands. It was fought in Ireland. In the summer of 1588 it was fought against the concentrated power of the Spanish Armada near the south coast of England.

The story of the attack and defeat of the Spanish Armada in 1588 has been oft told and well told, for it has all the qualities of high drama: the brilliant display of cool seamanship in the channel; the climactic moment of the assembly of English manhood in defence of the queen's person at Tilbury, and finally the anti-climax of weakness and disaster which overtook victor and vanquished alike. To understand what happened we must recognise that there was strength, skill and devotion on both sides; but the English had a more modern fleet and could call upon a measure of independence and imagination which the Spanish admirals, held fast by the tight strategy of their king, could not command. No less important, although the Spaniards fought bravely, inspired by empire and religion, the English drove forward under the still greater inspiration of defence of their homeland. For they could see the green coasts, the golden bays and the white cliffs as they fought.

While some fought at sea, others gathered on land during those intoxicating days when they hastened in from the shires to Tilbury – some came dancing in – to defend the queen. Here surely was something to talk about in the long unrewarding years to follow. We do not know whether Shakespeare, on the brink of his great career, witnessed any of these scenes; but I take from him the description of another famous day, only because I know of nothing better to capture the mood of this later occasion. For this surely was the St Crispin's day of the Elizabethans:

> He that outlives this day and comes safe home
> Will stand a tip-toe when this day is named . . .
> He that shall live this day, and see old age,
> Will yearly, on the vigil, feast his neighbours . . .
> This story shall the good man teach his son . . .
> From this day to the ending of the world.

The memories of that late summer of 1588 have blotted out the long years of war and disappointment which followed. Great though the victory was, it has distorted the pattern of events. The defeat of the Armada did not mean that the enemy had been destroyed. It was, in the Churchillian phrase, not the beginning of the end, but the end of the beginning. It showed, as did the Battle of Britain in the opening phase of the Second World War, that the enemy was not invincible. It lent courage to the forces of resistance. It argued, not only that tyranny *should* be resisted, but that it *could* be resisted. What it did not reveal was the length of the struggle and the price it would charge.

It was not in the nature of the Spaniard to acknowledge defeat, or of the Englishman to renounce the hopes of an enduring victory. So the war dragged on in several theatres and was fought most bitterly in Ireland, whose desperate people constantly awaited the Spanish liberator; for a new Armada was always in prospect. As late as 1597 an invasion fleet was assembled – to be broken by the winds off the north-western coast of France. At which harbour or invasion area it was aimed we do not know; but the commander was given a freedom of manoeuvre which his predecessor in 1588 would have envied from the bottom of his heart. A Spanish document, drawn up for the Spanish admiral of 1597, has recently come to light; and it is especially interesting for giving a foreign impression of this country.[1] Here, for example, is the description of Milford Haven in Wales:

'It is a protected harbour and is six or seven leagues round about.

There is room for countless ships.

There is no fortress, and but one tower at the entrance. On the right side it is not strong, it usually has two pieces of artillery, which cannot prevent an entry. It is six leagues to the head of the river. There is an open village.

It has water, meat and grain in abundance.

There are many Catholics and the people are naturally enemies of the English and do not speak their language.'

The war continued . . .

If war is political argument extended over many spheres, then one of these spheres was Parliament. Essential to success in war was success in war finance,

[1] A. J. Loomie, 'An Armada pilot's survey of the English coastline, October, 1597' (*Mariner's Mirror* (1963)), xlix, 288–300.

and the key to war finance was held by Parliament. Here was the force behind the whole constitutional challenge to the high authority of Elizabeth, a challenge which was to overwhelm the second of her successors. The assumptions of Elizabethan peace finance had been that the normal crown revenues from land, and the traditional import and export duties, with a few other items, would suffice to pay for the normal costs of government. In times of war or danger, extraordinary necessity would be met, at least partly, by extraordinary grants of taxation by Parliament. We must never lose sight of the fact that they believed that parliamentary taxation was quite exceptional – in technical terms, extraordinary. Moreover, the House of Commons did not consist of a body of men whose sole object was to give the queen a full treasury and a tranquil mind. Not unreasonably, if they granted money they wanted to know how it was spent – and to have a share in spending it.

Not unreasonably . . .? We who write words such as these do so because the events since the English Revolution of 1641 have laid their stamp upon our minds and attitudes. We think in terms of a constitutional monarchy with the executive answerable to Parliament. By contrast, the Elizabethan Parliaments still bore the shape of their medieval moulds. They were intended to be advisory bodies, rarely summoned and quickly sped on their way again. The queen herself reminded members that she had rarely assembled them in Parliament; and this she took to be a virtue. It was an opinion, however, which was shared by a diminishing number of her parliamentarians. By now, many of them wanted to come because they felt that they had something to do. And when they came, they were not prepared tamely to grant whatever was asked. They often granted less than was called for and less speedily that it was needed. And they improved upon the occasion by asking that certain financial grievances, for example abuses of wardship and monopolies, should be redressed. They offered advice also on a lot of other subjects upon which the queen considered that they were neither well-informed nor helpful, and sometimes not even friendly.

The queen took her stand on her inherited power, a power which acknowledged no superior on earth and did not share its authority in the making of war or the settling of peace, in governing the church or managing the state. Many parliamentarians accepted this doctrine, and even those who did not went through the motions of appearing to accept it. But these gestures were being emptied of much of their content. How could such able and experienced men of the world continue to believe that the repository of all political wisdom lay in an ageing queen, helped by a handful of overworked ministers, who had long ago grown stale in the exacting tedium of daily administration? The performance of the ministers during these last dark years of the reign was neither efficient nor edifying; and the queen herself had endured the burdens of governance for too long and remorseless a time. When, in 1601, the parliamentarians disputed, not only monopolies, but the very essence of sovereignty itself, they found monarch and ministers alike in disarray. The M.P.s were tired of petitions which they had the right to present but which the queen had the right to ignore. They wanted an Act of Parliament prepared and passed by them to which the queen must one way or another be forced to assent. They decided to take the initiative, in essence to challenge the sovereignty of the crown.

Long before that fatal moment was reached, the queen had yielded. If this was what contemporaries called love-play, then it was the kind of love-play from which one of the participants retired hurt. In theory the queen had not yielded a single fragment of her sovereign rights, for her prompt cancellation of many of the offending monopolies rendered an Act of Parliament super-fluous. But still she had yielded.

The results of this dispute are sometimes thought of as a compromise. But this was no compromise. By defini-tion, a compromise is something in which both sides give up, in practice or theory, some of their claims. In practice the queen had been forced to give up one of her sovereign rights, namely that of granting monopolies as and when and to whom she pleased. The Commons had had nothing to lose and they had given up nothing. 'The King,' Tyndale had written on the eve of the Reformation, in 1528, 'is in this world without law, and may at his own lust do right and wrong and shall give accounts to God only.' A lot had happened since 1528 and there was plenty more to come. 'I am surprised,' remarked James I of Parliament, as much in sorrow as in anger, 'that my ancestors should ever have permitted such an institution to come in existence. I am a stranger and found it here when I arrived, so that I am obliged to put up with what I cannot get rid of.'

Poverty corrodes power. It is always so. And when the power is that of monarchy, then it is especially vulnerable. Wealthy rulers rarely summon popular assemblies because they do not want to share power, and have no need to. But the queen was now in acute financial difficulties. It is of the year 1601 that the latest student of the Elizabethan Exchequer, Dr R. B. Outhwaite, writes[1]

The crown was deep in debt: Elizabeth owed the Corpora-tion [of London] £80,000, and had failed to pay the interest charges on the last loan, and a further £120,000 was out-standing on privy seal loans. Crown lands were being sold on an unprecedented scale and the proceeds were being used, not to repay these debts, but to keep the crown's head above the continuously high level of expenditure. Moreover, the queen

[1] R. B. Outhwaite, 'Studies in Elizabethan Government Finance' (Unpublished Nottingham Ph.D. thesis, 1964), p. 22.

was old, there were doubts about the succession, and there was never any guarantee that her successor would honour her debts. These factors combined to produce a situation in which Elizabeth's credit reached its nadir.

No wonder Elizabeth yielded on monopolies. An immediate grant of taxation was urgent, and she bowed to necessity.

But in other spheres the queen did not yield. Throughout her reign she had functioned through a divided ministry. The notion of collective cabinet responsibility dates of course from the eighteenth century and is a token of the strength of the office of the prime minister who presides at its meetings. By contrast, the fact that the ministries of the earlier centuries were divided reveals the strength of the monarch. Each minister was separately answerable to the king and to no one else; and no single one of the ministers was supreme. If Elizabeth believed in the balance of power abroad, she believed equally strongly in the balance of power at home. 'The principal note of her reign,' wrote Sir Robert Naunton, her contemporary, 'will be that she ruled much by faction and parties which she herself both made, upheld and weakened, as her own great judgment advised.' Her ministers, he said, 'were never more than tenants-at-will'. There was no prime minister, and it would be an anachronism to expect one.

Her ministers tacitly acknowledged the situation even though they chafed under the control. In these later years one such minister, the Earl of Essex, handsome, bold, adventurous, a man whose ambition outran both his prudence and his skill, found the restraints intolerable. He represented, moreover, the war party who wanted a more vigorous prosecution of English aims; and in pressing for extreme action he found himself in conflict not only with the queen but with Burghley, the Lord Treasurer. There is a famous story of how Burghley at his last appearance at the queen's council in 1598 had opened a discussion about the possibility of a negotiated peace with Spain. At once the Earl of Essex made a strong plea that any such plan be rejected; and to this the aged Treasurer made a devastating reply, as he drew out his prayer book and pointed to a passage in the Book of Psalms. It reads: 'Bloody and deceitful men shall not live out half their days.'

Essex was 'too bold an engrosser both of fame and favour', Naunton tells us; or, as we should say, he wanted to gather all power into his own hands. He strove 'to over-rule all'. In this he was resisted by the queen and resisted also by the Cecils and their followers. Thus he stumbled into the self-destructive glory of being appointed supreme commander in Ireland at the lowest ebb of England's fortunes there. He failed as others had before him, and with it there failed his whole grasp on affairs. There followed a foolish and treasonable outbreak into which he was in part driven by his irresponsible followers. In 1601 he was executed.

An earlier chapter of this book is entitled the 'Dream of Order'. I might almost have called this one the 'Dream of Power'. If the Earl of Essex dreamed of power, which eluded him until the end, Christopher Marlowe's *Tamburlaine* and *Dr Faustus* each in their way recount the same dream. The Elizabethans were obsessed by power, power in words as much as power in politics. People said that all this came from Machiavelli whose wicked doctrines expounded the glory of political authority, drained of all morality – the same charge would be made against Thomas Hobbes and his *Leviathan* in the middle of the seventeenth century.

But if, like the queen, Elizabethans understood the splendours of power, they also like her knew its burdens – and its emptiness. 'There is in human nature generally more of the fool than of the wise,' wrote Francis Bacon in his essay *Of Boldness*, 'and therefore those faculties by which the foolish part of men's minds is taken are most potent.' By what means, he asks, can leaders hold their followers in subjection? He answers: 'What first? *boldness*; what second and third? – *boldness*' – that is the tawdry, aggressive grandeur of leadership. 'And yet boldness is a child of ignorance and baseness, far inferior to other parts. But nevertheless it doth fascinate, and bind hand and foot those that are either shallow in judgment or weak in courage, which are the greatest part; yea, and prevaileth with wise men at weak times.' In short, the exercise of political power and its enjoyment involves something of a confidence trick. But in another essay, *Of Great Place*, he presents the other side of the coin. 'Men in great place are thrice servants,' he writes, 'servants of the sovereign or state, servants of fame, and servants of business; so as they have no freedom, neither in their persons, nor in their actions, nor in their times.' 'It is a strange desire,' he adds drily, 'to seek power and to lose liberty; or to seek power over others, and to lose power over a man's self. The rising unto place is laborious, and by pains men come to greater pains. And it is sometimes base, and by indignities men come to dignities. The standing is slippery, and the regress is either a downfall, or at least an eclipse, which is a melancholy thing.' Bacon had been, at one time, a close adviser of the Earl of Essex; and he knew what he was talking about. He would experience all this to the full himself when he was driven from the high office of Lord Chancellor on the charge of corruption. Great persons, he says, 'had need to borrow other men's opinions to think themselves happy'.

But if so much in Bacon, Marlowe and Shakespeare is concerned with the exercise of power in politics, these writers were familiar also, as were many of their contemporaries, with power in other forms. In the world of religion, the authors of the 'Martin Marprelate' tracts were concerned to attack, as their pseudonym makes clear, the power of the bishop and to replace it with the spiritual commonwealth of the Puritans. In doing so these writers gave a sharp, rough cutting edge to English prose which could on occasion make it a deadly instrument in debate. The indomitable Peter Wentworth, fighting the same battle, in and out of Parliament, left his own indelible mark on polemical literature, as well as on the history of freedom of thought.

Other pressures were at work upon an older tradition of politics and society. Drake strove for the destruction of Spanish supremacy, Hawkins for a trading imperialism based on sea power, Ralegh for a colonial civilisation in the New World. These vast projects sank below the Atlantic, along with the battered ships which had borne them out to sea. But the experiments had been made, the theories tested and modified; and the children and grandchildren of the Elizabethans would, in their time, sail westwards to the established places of settlement overseas.

Meanwhile there was disappointment in many spheres; and the year 1601 had been the darkest year of a dark decade. Or so it would seem if we were to think solely in terms of the politics of the time, and of historical studies conceived only within the conventional political framework. Yet such a version would be incomplete and false. For this last decade, in spite of all the bitterness of its politics, and all its economic and social troubles, was the golden decade of English literature.

Even if, for the moment, we think only of prose, the evidence pours in of the ever-extending dimensions of Elizabethan literature: the fiction and autobiographical writings of Robert Greene; the documentary novels of Lodge and Deloney; the translations of Thomas North and the chronicles of Holinshed, both of them to be of immense value to Shakespeare; the historical writings of Camden and Stow; the brilliant satire of Nashe; and the magnificent narratives of naval exploits and exploration collected by Hakluyt – for now indeed English prose had spread its sails and taken to the sea. Nor should we forget the queen herself who, when moved in spirit, could write her instructions – and rebukes – in a trenchant, unambiguous prose.

There were other winds too, dispersing the accepted processes of thought and life. Perhaps one of the most striking examples of the new outlook, expressed in an extreme form, is in the work of Gabriel Harvey, that remote and ineffectual don at Cambridge, whose power over words vastly exceeded his power in any sphere of politics – including university politics, the most abased branch of that science.

Harvey rejected the notion that a golden age lay buried in the past: 'You suppose the first age was the golden age,' he wrote to his friend Edmund Spenser. 'It is nothing so.' He accused Spenser of believing that they now lived in

. . . a foolish mad world, wherein all things are over-ruled by fancy. What greater error? All things else are but trouble of mind and vexation of spirit. Until a man's fancy be satisfied, he wanteth his most sovereign contentment, and cannot be at quiet in himself. You suppose most of these bodily and sensual pleasures are to be abandoned as unlawful, and the inward contemplative delights of the mind more zealously to be embraced as most commendable.

Good Lord, you a gentleman, a courtier, a youth, and go about to revive so old and stale a bookish opinion, dead and buried many hundred years before you or I knew whether there were any world or no!

This was blatant and provocative. But it is in Ralegh and others that we meet, over and over again, the disturbed scepticism of the age.

In contrast we turn to William Harrison, the antiquary, for something of a quieter tradition both in the life and the prose of the Elizabethans:

For mine own part, good reader, let me boast a little of my garden which is but small, and the whole area thereof little above three hundred foot of ground. And yet, such hath been my good luck in purchase of the variety of simples [herbs] that, notwithstanding my small ability, there are very near three hundred of one sort and other contained therein, no one of them being common or usually to be had. If, therefore, my little plot, void of all cost in keeping, be so well furnished, what shall we think of those of Hampton Court, Nonesuch, Theobalds, Cobham garden. . . .?

Not all Elizabethan prose was simple, effective, graceful, powerful. Much of it, as we can see from many of the sermons and pamphlets which have survived, was turgid, ponderous, complex. But at its best it has never been surpassed. It was a living language of immense variety, freedom and scope, which the greatest writers explored and exploited to the full. Who is the greatest of them all? I do not know. But if a man were setting out for a distant place with room in his knapsack for only one small book, then the one that would serve him best would not be by Spenser or Shakespeare or Ralegh, for all their greatness, but the Essays of Francis Bacon, for here would be perfect prose written by an observer of genius.

Some of the outstanding prose writers, like Sidney and Ralegh, were also fine poets. Many of the courtiers like the Earl of Oxford, the Earl of Essex and Sir Edward Dyer wrote distinguished verse. It is said that even Robert Cecil wrote verse; but if it was as bad as the doggerel written by his father, Lord Treasurer Burghley, then its disappearance is no great loss to literature. Queen Elizabeth's own verse is better than that of her Lord Treasurer; but not much better. Robert Southwell, the Catholic priest and martyr, wrote some of the finest Elizabethan poetry while he was in prison. Poesie needed no longer a defence, for it seemed that a whole generation had burst into song; and in the last year of the century some of the best work of the age was gathered together in *Englands Helicon*, to be followed next year by Thomas Morley's *Triumphs of Oriana*, a collection of madrigals by various composers in honour of the queen. But the greatest poet of the time was also its greatest playwright; and it was through the theatre that Elizabethan culture exercised its most abiding influence.

The London theatre was the meeting ground of the playwrights, the courtiers and the ordinary citizens of the capital and its suburbs. It constantly renewed itself from the popular emotion; but its foundations lay deep in the medieval miracle and morality plays, in the student performances in the Inns of Court and in the aristocratic interludes in the houses of the nobility. For example, the earliest Elizabethan tragedy was probably *Gorbuduc*, acted before Queen Elizabeth at the Inner Temple in 1562, and written by Thomas Norton, one of the Puritan leaders of the House of Commons, and Thomas Sackville, who ended his career as Earl of Dorset and Lord Treasurer of England. The play was a jejune affair, but it marked a considerable advance upon its predecessors. The great flow of drama came later, in the fifteen eighties and nineties, as in the work of John Lyly who, as a prose writer, is remembered for his oppressive artificiality of style yet, as a playwright, for making prose a natural vehicle for expression, compared with the crude rhymes of the earlier comedies. Peele, Greene, Marlowe, Kyd, each added his own richness to the contemporary theatre, passing on to Shakespeare an audience and a tradition which now found its greatest voice.

It would be impossible, as well as absurd, to attempt here an assessment of Shakespeare's rôle in English literature. It is perhaps more useful, in this place, to embark on a lesser task, that is, to look at his work with the eye of an individual historian using his plays to learn something of his responses to the problems of his time.

It is sometimes said that Shakespeare's plays transcend time and space. That is of course true. He is a dramatist not a historian. But his problems are those of the historian; and he is free to go where he pleases. In that sense he transcends time and space. He can explore the problem of ambition and honour in the Rome of Julius Caesar, or the Scotland of Macbeth, or the England of Richard III. He is concerned with the problems of the demagogue and mob-rule in the Rome of Coriolanus. He can consider the appalling cost of civil strife in the England of Richard II or of his successors Henry IV, Henry V and Henry VI. He can display the impact of private emotions on public affairs in the Denmark of Hamlet or the Egypt of Cleopatra. But every one of these problems is acutely Elizabethan: ambition, honour, the appeal to the people – the Elizabethans called it popularity – war, the relations between private emotions and public affairs. No man, not even a genius, can wholly divest himself of time and place, cut himself off from his own generation. Shakespeare remained an Elizabethan.

Much of what we witness, for example, in the play *Richard III* is, of course, propaganda, although I do not think that Shakespeare was the propagandist. But his version of Richard III is based ultimately upon the work of Sir Thomas More, and More's account was derived mainly from Cardinal Morton. Morton was a minister of Henry VII, the first of the Tudors who, as Richmond, had defeated Richard III at the battle of Bosworth and taken his crown from him. So, to Henry VII, and to the Tudors and their supporters, Richard III was the arch-villain, the usurping tyrant, the wicked uncle who murdered the Princes in the Tower. All this Shakespeare accepts, and his play unfolds a terrible retribution for Richard III. But the historical and the topical are enlarged into the universal, into the tragedy of great power misused and itself destroyed; we have here that drastic change of fortune, that mutability, which is a recurrent theme in Elizabethan literature – and a familiar one in Tudor politics. Who, at the end of the play, if he recalls the brutality of Richard, fails to recall also the tragic courage of the man in his last hours?

> ... I have set my life upon a cast,
> And I will stand the hazard of the die!
> I think there be six Richmonds in the field;
> Five have I slain today instead of him.

Much that Shakespeare writes is inevitably concerned with war. Numerous examples come to the mind, from which we choose *Hamlet*, which belongs to the end of the reign. In one scene we meet Fortinbras, king of Norway, about to lead an army of men against Poland. Hamlet asks a captain of the invading forces what is the object of the campaign, and he answers:

> Truly to speak, and with no addition
> We go to gain a little patch of ground
> That hath in it no profit but the name.
> To pay five ducats, five, I would not farm it.

'Why then,' says Hamlet, 'the Polack never will defend it.' But the captain answers: 'Yes, 'tis already garrisoned.' And, shortly afterwards, Hamlet comments:

>   ... I see
> The imminent death of twenty thousand men,
> That, for a fantasy and trick of fame,
> Go to their graves like beds.

Here, as in so much else, Shakespeare looks back over centuries of warfare and over his own lifetime – and anticipates the centuries to come. He does not say that war is wrong. He never crosses the boundary from drama to ideological propaganda. But he says that this is how men have behaved in history: they have destroyed each other by the thousand for some barren patch of frontier land not worth five ducats a year. They have gone to their graves like beds for some irrelevant slogan or some momentary prestige. They have followed men like Fortinbras, King of Norway, without thinking what lay before them at the end of the road.

Even the centuries-old enmity between England and France is displayed as something futile, wasteful, fruitless: peace is long overdue. In the play of that name, Henry v marries the daughter of the French king and it is the French king who expresses, according to Shakespeare, the widespread hope that:

> . . . the contending kingdoms
> Of France and England, whose very shores look pale
> With envy of each other's happiness,
> May cease their hatred, and this dear conjunction
> Plant neighbourhood and Christian-like accord
> In their sweet bosoms, that never war advance
> His bleeding sword twixt England and fair France.

And to this all say 'Amen!'

But it is civil war that Shakespeare most vividly displays in the futility of its horror. In the play *Henry VI* he makes the king himself lament the terrible times when father and son slay each other. In the last speech in *Richard III*, he reverts to the same theme:

> England hath long been mad, and scarr'd herself;
> The brother blindly shed the brother's blood,
> The father rashly slaughter'd his own son;
> The son, compell'd, been butcher to the sire.

Can anyone have forgotten the Wars of the Roses, the dark shadow which lay across the whole Tudor inheritance?

Many other examples could be given of Shakespeare's detached involvement in the problems of his day. In Ulysses' famous speech in *Troilus and Cressida* he raises questions about the dissolution of the existing social framework. Even *Much Ado*, in its antics of Dogberry and Verges, has something, albeit amusing, about poverty and vagrancy; and it is said again more sharply in *Henry VIII* and *Timon of Athens*. All the historical plays and many of the tragedies raise searching questions about the nature of political power, the subject which was to dominate the large controversies of the seventeenth century. It may well be true, as Dr Johnson tells us, that Shakespeare 'seems to write without any moral purpose'; but he is always confronting us with the major moral issues, those same issues which ever engage the mind of the historian.

If then we revert to the old question: does Shakespeare give us a true version of history? the answer is surely no. Shakespeare tampers with the chronology as often as he wants to. He telescopes events for dramatic purposes and re-moulds character for the same ends. He is blatantly anachronistic, for his Romans are Elizabethans in fancy dress. But these qualities, which would be unpardonable in the historian, are tolerable and perhaps essential in the dramatist. For Shakespeare sees his events *sub specie aeternitatis*. He sees not only a man but all men; not only a crucial moment in the history of a nation but the timeless drama of all nations.

In the historical context, therefore, his work must always be used with the greatest caution. Yet no historian coming away from one of his plays, however many times he may have seen it, and whatever its theme, fails to bring with him some additional thread from the texture of the Elizabethan past. To the present writer, Shakespeare's works will always remain one of the primary sources for an understanding of Elizabethan society.

Hence we find in Shakespeare echoes of these dark years – the 'declination of the times' as a contemporary called it – but he conveys also much of the high comedy, the gay courage of his contemporaries. The queen's own life had always displayed a compound of these changing moods; and men who knew her until her seventieth year testified to the vigour of her enjoyment of life, almost to the end. But in the early months of 1603 the fatigues of war, of solitary government over more than four decades, of disappointment, obliterated for the time being her sense of the rich achievements of her reign. She was very tired and there was little more that she could do. Here is one of the best descriptions of her passing. It is by the diarist, John Manningham, who on the 24th March 1603 entered in his book: 'This morning about three at clock Her Majesty departed this life, mildly like a lamb, easily like a ripe apple from the tree.' For her, ripeness was all.

V

The Elizabethan Nation
Some Historical Problems

It is impossible to study the Elizabethan nation without studying the queen who reigned over them. 'Both in her life and her death,' said her contemporary, Thomas Dekker, 'she was appointed to be the mirror of her time.' The trouble is that she not only mirrored her own time but all time. From her day onwards she has reflected back to historians many of the notions they brought with them to their task. For example, James Anthony Froude, one of the great nineteenth-century historians, had begun work on the Tudor period with an admiration for Elizabeth. By the end, all that was over. 'The private letters which passed between him (Burghley) and Walsingham about Elizabeth,' he wrote to a correspondent, 'have destroyed finally the prejudice that still clung to me that, notwithstanding her many faults, she was a woman of ability. Evidently in their opinion she had no ability at all worth calling by the name.' In his *History of England* the same thing is said, in a famous passage:

Vain as she was of her own sagacity, she never modified a course recommended to her by Burghley without injury both to the realm and to herself. She never chose an opposite course without plunging into embarrassments from which his skill and Walsingham's were barely able to extricate her. The good results of her reign were the fruits of a policy which was not her own, and which she starved and mutilated when energy and completeness were most needed.

Of Lord Burghley, he said elsewhere, in a private letter,

'He, it is more and more clear to me, was the solitary author of Elizabeth's and England's greatness.'

Froude is, of course, an extreme example. Deeply involved as he was in the events of his own day, including the Catholic revival – to which he was bitterly opposed – he saw Elizabeth as betraying the just cause by her relative moderation to the Catholics. But the very fact that Froude is such an extreme case reminds us that biography is a subjective thing.

All biography is distortion. However historically well-founded his work may be, the biographer takes a man out of his context, and in so doing is forced to alter the focus of the age. It reminds one of the use made by some newspapers of the photograph of a group of young men, when one of them has since become famous. His photograph is cut out from the rest and enlarged. The result is either a flat portrait deprived of the vitality of the group as a whole, or else he emerges as larger than life, his features gross and exaggerated, out of all proportion. In any case, this is not the man he was.

This will seem strange doctrine, coming from one who has written one biography and is engaged in writing another. But because an art form is imperfect, that is no reason for not practising it. The biographer, conscious of the hazards of his methods, may yet contribute to historical understanding. For he looks at the past from within the life and mind of a single person. If he can, however briefly, establish an intimate contact with a man or woman of a past generation, then he adds something living to his analysis of society, which is his principal function as a historian.

By contemporaries, Elizabeth was vilified and adored, cursed and blessed; and the process has ever continued. It is a difficult task to isolate her from her admirers no less than from her detractors. She was not all wise, all patient, all virtuous. She did not accurately assess all future political developments and take appropriate steps.

Who could? She blundered, she grew impatient, she saddled her ministers with the blame for her own failings. She was unsparing – and sometimes cruelly unfunny – in her wit. She could arouse warm emotions on her progresses among her people; but to those who knew her well she must have been a difficult person to love.

Yet when all is said, she tried hard to heal the wounds and divisions of the England she inherited, and she met with a large measure of success. She was a divided person, torn between the individual, private interests of a highly intelligent, vigorous woman and the public tasks which denied her the full enjoyment and expression of her private being. In her public tasks she succeeded admirably during the first thirty years of her reign in healing the wounds and binding the nation to her own purposes; but she failed significantly during the last fifteen. Delay, ambiguity, the elevation of monarchy to raise the aims and unify the purpose of the Elizabethan people were no longer enough. In one sense her reign was both too long and too short. If she had lived ten years less she might have gone down to history as the most successful monarch to sit on the English throne. If she could possibly have lived ten years longer we should perhaps have known the answer to some of the problems of her reign which still elude us; for their issue could not have been long delayed. In many respects the year 1603 does not end an epoch. The Tudor system survived for another forty years; but even before she died it had already started to break down.

How far, then, were the problems of the early Stuarts theirs or Elizabeth's. For example, we know that the Puritan opposition which had been a thorn in her flesh almost from the beginning of the reign, grew in the 1570s more intense, in and out of Parliament, and flared up in an extreme form at the time of the Martin Marprelate tracts in 1588–9. Yet it seems to have died down, at least in Parliament, in the last decade of her reign. Had it, in fact, died down, and, if so, why did it revive so speedily under James I? We shall know more about this when we have one day plotted our map showing the extent of Puritanism – and Catholicism – in England. How Catholic was Lancashire, how Protestant was Essex? We can only guess. We know too that in the early seventeenth century the political opposition was most powerfully directed against the extension of crown revenue, and against the prerogative courts. Could Elizabeth have contained the opposition much longer? These questions, a few among many, are not mere speculative ones for they raise the whole issue of Elizabeth's authority and power. In short, what power did she enjoy and what was its relation to the social structure of the nation?

This is the most absorbing of all the Tudor problems. Yet here we labour under the gravest handicaps. When Froude said that Burghley was 'the solitary author of Elizabeth's and England's greatness', he was exceeding his brief. He did not have the material on which to base this judgment. Nor have we. The process by which the government will is formulated and transmitted is one of the toughest historical questions to answer. It is still openly debated as to how it is done even in our own day. It is incomparably more obscure in a time of personal monarchy. The important decisions are given by word of mouth and may be the result, sometimes, of protracted discussions between monarch and ministers. All the preparatory work is done by the minister and the papers show his hand. But who initiated the enquiry and who was responsible for the final decision? Did the minister persuade and press the monarch or did the monarch direct the minister? We are in a world of shadows. Yet these problems do exercise the historian, although contemporaries rarely see the questions so precisely – and perhaps misleadingly – defined.

In the Elizabethan period we are faced with two additional difficulties. There is evidence that Burghley, who was the queen's closest adviser for forty years, engaged in some deliberate destruction of his papers – and that was not in order to save space! Secondly, he went out of his way to imply that he was a mere servant of the queen, with the minimum of powers, and that these powers consisted mostly of taking the unpopular responsibility for refusing suitors for royal favours. What in fact went on behind this smoke-screen of Burghley's it is hard to say. Contemporaries believed with Spenser that this whole picture was false, that Burghley monopolised power and barred other men from sharing it, that he was

> . . . like an aged tree
> Lets none shoot up that nigh him planted be.

No one can ever again wholly accept Froude's theory – which is very much the same as Spenser's but expressed in favourable terms to Burghley – since the appearance of Sir John Neale's masterly investigation of the Elizabethan Parliaments. In two spheres in particular, in the queen's resolution to stand fast to prevent the establishment of a Puritan church, and in her defence of Mary, Queen of Scots, it is now clear that she stood out against many of her advisers and parliamentarians, in the one case successfully, in the other failing only after a long struggle. If now we can by some process discover more about the formulation of *economic* policy, the handling of revenue, and the contemporary concepts of law and the constitution, then an answer to our question will be in sight.

Meanwhile, other questions press for an answer. We know that, less than forty years after the death of the queen, England was divided in civil war. Did the divisions have their origins in the Elizabethan period, in some inherent tension between the government and society, or perhaps within society itself? This is no occasion to re-open the dead controversy over the gentry. It is indeed hard to recall that there was a time when the streets of Oxford ran with blood (or printer's ink: it is sometimes hard to tell the difference) on this burning issue. For men were prepared to lay down their (academic) lives in defence of their exposed positions.

But if the argument no longer stirs us, the whole debate was entirely beneficial for Tudor studies. Professor R. H. Tawney, who started it, saw in land the roots of power. He therefore analysed the rise of a new class of middling landowners, between aristocracy and yeomanry, who extended their territories and modernised their use. Rising to economic power, they sought to express it politically – in other words, to control policy and government – and ran headlong into the entrenched resistance of the Stuart monarchy, a monarchy allied with that section of the aristocracy which had not marched with the times. Such a situation finally deteriorated into civil war. We cannot, of course, summarise in a few lines a brilliant piece of historical analysis, nor the brilliance of the counter-offensive launched by Professor Hugh Trevor-Roper. Challenging Tawney in both his methods and his conclusions, Mr Trevor-Roper rejected the concept of the gentry class as an entity. To him the division of England came, not over land, but over office, that is office of profit and patronage under the crown. The government had thousands of appointments at its disposal; and the sweets of office tempted all men. Access to office could mean both wealth and power, for the government service was vast, influential and ever-growing; exclusion could mean exclusion from both wealth and power, whether one belonged to the gentry or not. To him this division separated the 'ins' from the 'outs', the holders of government office from the opposition.

Here then was a confrontation between two of the most distinguished historians of the time, historians whose methods had much more in common than either might have been prepared to acknowledge. There is no question that the gentry as a class, or more likely a congeries of groups, formed an important element of the English social structure of the time and for long afterwards. There can be no question also that in the use and abuse of office lies the explanation of major aspects of Tudor society and its inner conflicts. But this is not to say that the resolution of the gentry controversy is some vague compromise; rather, that starting from the questions raised we are beginning – but only just beginning – to go forward to a detailed analysis of the social order. This has forced historians and their students to look searchingly at the monarch and Parliament, at administration and patronage. It has made them go out into the shires because the answers to these questions lie only partly in London; the remainder will be found in provincial England. London represented probably no more than one twentieth of the population as a whole.

But the population of London was still growing. In the reign of Elizabeth it had doubled, reaching about 200,000 by the end. The Thames, on which it stood, was the main artery of southern England. It was the Thames of Spenser's *Prothalamion* –

> . . . the shore of silver streaming Thames,
> Whose rutty bank the which his river hems,
> Was painted all with variable flowers,
> And all the meads adorned with dainty gems,
> Fit to deck maidens' bowers . . .

But it was also the Thames which De Maisse, ambassador of France, saw and described in 1597. 'From Greenwich to London,' he wrote, 'it is a magnificent sight to see the number of ships and boats which lie in anchor, insomuch that for two leagues you see nothing but ships that serve as well for war as for traffic.'

William Camden, historian of Elizabethan England, declared that London was 'the epitome of all Britain, the seat of the British Empire'. In James I, it aroused other emotions. Alarmed at the size and growth of his capital he urged parliamentarians and others, as soon as their business was over, to pack up and go home – and to take their wives and daughters with them. His capital continued to grow.

London was the centre of politics, of administration, of religion, of law, of commerce. It was the social centre for the leading men of the age, with their great houses along the Thames. It was a great cultural centre with its Inns of Court, its theatres, its Chapel Royal. It was a pioneer in social welfare with its Christ's Hospital, dealing with the care and education for poor children, St Bartholomew's for the sick, St Mary Bethlehem (Bedlam) for the mentally sick; it had its Bridewell workhouse, and its system of local taxation to pay for this and much else. All this was consolidated on a national scale in the great statutes of 1598. But London remained a great slum, over-crowded, poverty stricken, diseased, which like a giant mantis spider killed off many thousands of those who were drawn in fascination towards her.

Where did they all come from? This is a large question of social geography which cries aloud for investigation, and with it the whole problem of the continued rise in population during the early decades of the seventeenth century.

And beyond these lie the massive problems of price revolutions, standards of living, social values, political aims. To these great and fascinating issues historians and their students are increasingly directing their minds.

The history of the Elizabethan nation is not just the history of a queen, of her government, of her politics, of the economic system, but of a whole society of diverse people, responding to the pressures of new experiences in all aspects of their lives. It is the history of their developing culture and their intercourse with the civilisation of Europe. It is the history of their religious faiths and affiliations. It is the history of their social assumptions, their system of patronage, their attitudes to war and peace, to this world and the next. History is extending its frontiers. Many of us now regard these aspects of the past – which earlier historians would have banished to other disciplines – as inherent to our studies. We hold that *'nihil humani alienum'* – nothing involving man is outside our range.

One of the most stimulating things about the Elizabethan period is therefore the enormous prospects it offers for the exploration of new lines of development by means of entirely new historical methods. For we are only at the beginning of knowledge. 'Histories,' says Francis Bacon, 'make men wise.' Faced with so many questions about the Elizabethan period which remain unanswered, one adds that history makes men humble. Or at least, it should do.

Appendix 1

A Calendar of Events

1558 Loss of Calais
Death of Mary Tudor (Nov. 17), accession of Elizabeth I. William Cecil (later Lord Burghley) appointed Secretary of State (Nov. 20)

1559 Treaty of Cateau-Cambrésis
Acts of Uniformity and Supremacy

1560 War in Scotland, ending in Treaty of Edinburgh and withdrawal of French troops

1561 Francis Bacon born

1562 Re-opening of Council of Trent
Beginning of French Wars of Religion
Publication of Jewel's *Apologia pro Ecclesia Anglicana*
Elizabeth I seriously ill with smallpox

1563 Concluding session of Council of Trent
Issue of Thirty-Nine Articles of Anglican Church
John Foxe's *Acts and Monuments* (i.e. 'Book of Martyrs') published

1564 Shakespeare, Marlowe, Galileo born. Death of Michelangelo

1568 Outbreak of Revolt of the Netherlands
Flight of Mary, Queen of Scots, to England

1569 Rebellion of the North

1570 Bull of Excommunication against Elizabeth I

1571 Ridolfi Plot

1572 Massacre of St Bartholomew's Day

1573? Ben Jonson born

1576 *The Theatre* built

1577 Beginning of Drake's voyage round the world
The Curtain built

1579 Spenser's *Shephearde's Calendar* published

1580 Completion of Drake's voyage round the world

1584 Assassination of William of Orange

1585 English expedition to Netherlands under Earl of Leicester
Beginning of war with Spain (ended 1604)
Act expelling Catholic priests from England

1586 Babington Plot. Trial of Mary, Queen of Scots

1587 Execution of Mary, Queen of Scots

1588 Defeat of Spanish Armada
Beginning of 'Martin Marprelate' controversy

1589 Hakluyt's *Principal Navigations* published
(*From the early 1590s Shakespeare was at work in London but the date of the production of his first play is not known*)

1593 Death of Marlowe

1597 First edition of Bacon's *Essays* published

1598 Death of Philip ii and Lord Burghley
End of French Civil War. Edict of Nantes (tolerating Huguenots) issued by Henri iv

1599 *Globe Theatre* opened
Death of Edmund Spenser. Birth of Oliver Cromwell

1601 Rebellion of Earl of Essex
William Gilbert's *De Magnete* published

1603 Death of Queen Elizabeth (March 24)

Appendix 2
Suggestions for further reading

The following titles provide no more than a brief, personal selection from a vast, and ever-growing, body of literature on the Elizabethan period. Full lists for all fields will be found in:

READ, c. ed. *Bibliography of British history, Tudor period*, O.U.P., 2nd edn. 1959. *63s*

GENERAL INTRODUCTORY WORKS

BINDOFF, S. T., *Tudor England* (Pelican history of England, vol. 5). Penguin Books, 1950. *3s 6d*

BLACK, J. B., *The reign of Elizabeth*, 1558–1603 (Oxford history of England, vol. 8), O.U.P., 2nd edn. 1959. *38s*

ELTON, G. R., *England under the Tudors*, Methuen, 1955. *25s*

NEALE, J. E., *Essays in Elizabethan history*, Cape, 1958. *21s* Paperback edn. with title *The age of Catharine de Medici and essays in Elizabethan history*, 1963. *10s 6d*

ROWSE, A. L., *The England of Elizabeth*, Macmillan, 1950. *35s*; paperback, *18s*

BINDOFF, S. T. and others, *eds. Elizabethan government and society*, Athlone Press, 1961. *50s*

FROUDE, J. A., *History of England from the fall of Wolsey to the defeat of the Spanish Armada*, 1856, 12 vols. Various editions

CHEYNEY, E. P., *A history of England from the defeat of the Spanish Armada to the death of Queen Elizabeth*, 2 vols. New York: 1914–1926. Gloucester, Mass.: Peter Smith, repr. 1949. 2 vols., $13

DODD, A. H., *Life in Elizabethan England*, Batsford, 1961. *21s*

THE CONSTITUTION AND POLITICAL THOUGHT

HOLDSWORTH, W. S., *History of English law*, Methuen, vol. iv, 3rd edn. 1937, o.p. vol. v, 3rd edn. 1947, o.p.

NEALE, J. E., *The Elizabethan House of Commons*, Cape, 1949. *35s*; Penguin Books, *15s*

NEALE, J. E., *Elizabeth I and her parliaments*, 1559–1601, Cape, vol. 1, 1953. 35s. vol. 2, 1957. 35s; paperback, 1965. 15s ea. vol.

WILLIAMS, P., *The Council in the Marches of Wales under Elizabeth I*, Cardiff: Wales U.P., 1958. 42s

REID, R. R., *The King's council in the north*, Longmans, 1921. o.p.

TILLYARD, E. W. M., *Elizabethan world picture*, Chatto & Windus, 1943. 12s 6d. Penguin Books, 6s

ALLEN, J. W., *A history of political thought in the sixteenth century*, Methuen, 3rd edn. 1957. 25s; paperback, 12s 6d

MORRIS, G., *Political thought in England: Tyndale to Hooker* (Home university library), O.U.P., 1953. 10s 6d

Sources

ELTON, G. R., *ed. The Tudor constitution: documents and commentary*, C.U.P., 1960. 52s 6d; paperback, 27s 6d

SMITH, SIR THOMAS, *De republica anglorum: a discourse on the Commonwealth of England*; ed. by L. Alston, C.U.P., 1906. o.p.

ECONOMIC AND SOCIAL PROBLEMS

CLARK, G. N., *The wealth of England*, 1496–1760 (Home university library), O.U.P., 1946. 10s 6d

FISHER, F. J., *ed. Essays in the economic and social history of Tudor and Stuart England in honour of R.H. Tawney*, C.U.P., 1961. 30s

RAMSEY, P., *Tudor economic problems*, Gollancz, 1963. 13s 6d

RAMSEY, G. D., *English overseas trade during the centuries of emergence*, Macmillan, 1957. 35s

WILLAN, T. S., *Studies in Elizabethan foreign trade*, Manchester U.P., 1959. 35s

BOWDEN, P. J., *The wool trade in Tudor and Stuart England*, Macmillan, 1962. 35s

TAWNEY, R. H., *The agrarian problem in the sixteenth century*, Longmans, 1912. o.p.

THIRSK, J., *Tudor enclosures*, Historical Association, 1959. 2s 6d

HOSKINS, W. G., *Provincial England: essays in social and economic history*, Macmillan, 1963. 42s
(See also his other collections of essays on local history)
DIETZ, F. C., *English public finance*, Vol. 2 1558–1641, 2nd edn. Cass, 1964. 55s
The discussions of the gentry problem by R. H. Tawney, H. Trevor-Roper, L. Stone and others can be followed in detail in the issues of the *Economic History Review* from 1941 onwards, supplemented by:
HEXTER, J. H., *Reappraisals in history*, Longmans, 1961. 30s
SIMPSON, A., *The wealth of the gentry*, C.U.P., 1961. 35s

Source

TAWNEY, R. H. and POWER, E., *eds. Tudor economic documents* Longmans, 1924. 3 vols. 80s

MILITARY, NAVAL AND OVERSEAS DEVELOPMENTS

TAYLOR, E. G. R., *Tudor geography*, 1485–1583, Methuen, 1930. o.p.
WILLIAMSON, J. A., *The age of Drake*, Black, 4th edn., 1961. 30s
CRUICKSHANK, C. G., *Elizabeth's army*, O.U.P., 1946. o.p.
MATTINGLY, G., *Defeat of the Spanish Armada*, Cape, 1959. 35s. Penguin Books, 8s 6d

RELIGION

There is no recent history of the Elizabethan church. Still valuable are:

FRERE, W. H., *History of the English Church, reigns of Elizabeth and James I*, Macmillan, 1904. o.p.
MEYER, A. O., *England and the Catholic Church under Queen Elizabeth*, K. Paul, 1916. o.p.
KNAPPEN, M. M., *Tudor puritanism: a chapter in the history of idealism*, University of Chicago P., 1939. o.p.
THOMPSON, J. V. P., *Supreme governor*, S.P.C.K., 1940. o.p.
JORDAN, W. K., *The development of religious toleration in England: from the beginning of the English Reformation to the death of Queen Elizabeth*, Allen & Unwin, 1932. o.p.

[HILL, J. E.] C., *Economic problems of the Church from Archbishop Whitgift to the Long Parliament*, O.U.P., 1956. 45s

BIOGRAPHIES

NEALE, J. E., *Queen Elizabeth I*, Cape, 1934. 30s; Penguin Books, 5s

HURSTFIELD, J., *Elizabeth I and the unity of England* (Teach yourself history library), English U.P., 1960. 12s 6d

STRONG, R. C., *Portraits of Queen Elizabeth I*, O.U.P., 1963. 42s

See also YATES, F. A., 'Queen Elizabeth as Astraea' in *Journal of the Warburg and Courtauld Institute* (1947)

HENDERSON, T. F., *Mary, Queen of Scots, her environment and tragedy*, Hutchinson, 1905. 2 vols., o.p.

WILLSON, D. H., *King James VI and I*, Cape, 1956. 30s. paperback, 12s 6d

READ, C., *Mr Secretary Cecil and Queen Elizabeth*, Cape, 1955. 35s

READ, C., *Lord Burghley and Queen Elizabeth*, Cape, 1960. 55s

READ, C., *Mr Secretary Walsingham and the policy of Queen Elizabeth*, O.U.P., 1925. 3 vols., o.p.

DEWAR, M., *Sir Thomas Smith: a Tudor intellectual in office*, Athlone P. 1964. 35s

STONE, L., *An Elizabethan: Sir Horatio Palavicino*, O.U.P., 1956. 45s

WILLIAMS, N., *Thomas Howard, fourth Duke of Norfolk*, Barrie & Rockliff, 1964. 35s

CULTURE

MERCER, E., *English art, 1553–1625*, O.U.P., 1962. 55s

BUXTON, J., *Elizabethan taste*, Macmillan, 1963. 35s

AUERBACH, E., *Tudor artists*, Athlone P. 1954. 70s

WOODFILL, W. L., *Musicians in English society from Elizabeth to Charles I*, Princeton U.P., O.U.P., 1953. o.p.

LEWIS, C. S., *English literature in the sixteenth century excluding drama*, O.U.P., 1954, 42s

WRIGHT, L. B., *Middle-class culture in Elizabethan England*, North Carolina Press, 1935; repr. Cornell U.P., 1964. $7.50

ONIONS, C. T., and others, *eds. Shakespeare's England*, O.U.P., 1916, 2 vols., 80s

SUTHERLAND, J. R. and HURSTFIELD, J., *eds. Shakespeare's world* E. Arnold, 1964. 25s

FORD, B., *ed. The age of Shakespeare* (Pelican guide to English literature, vol. 2). Penguin Books, 1955. 6s

WRIGHT, L. B. and LAMAR, V. A., *eds. Life and letters in Tudor and Stuart England*, N.Y.: Cornell U.P., 1962. 48s

HALL, A. R., *The scientific revolution*, 1500–1800, Longmans, 2nd edn. 1962. 30s; paperback, 15s

SINGER, C. and others, *eds. A history of technology, vol. 3. From the Renaissance to the Industrial Revolution*, O.U.P., 1957. £8 8s

Sources

MUIR, K. A., *ed. Elizabethan and Jacobean prose* 1550–1620 (Pelican books of English prose, ed. by K. Allott, vol. 1). Penguin Books, 1956. o.p.

HAYDN, H. C., *ed. Portable Elizabethan reader*, N. Y. Viking, 1955, $2.50

CHAMBERS, E. K., *ed. Oxford book of sixteenth century verse*, O.U.P., 1932. 25s

BACON, F., *Essays* 1597–1626, Dent, 1906. 8s 6d. Everyman paperback, 4s

WILSON, J. D., *Life in Shakespeare's England*, C.U.P., 1944. o.p.

INDEX